Center for Basque Studies
Basque Classics Series, No. 8

Linguæ Vasconum Primitiæ

The First Fruits of the Basque Language, 1545

Bernard Etxepare

Foreword by
Pello Salaburu

Introduction by
Beñat Oyharçabal

Translated by
Mikel Morris Pagoeta

Center for Basque Studies
University of Nevada, Reno
Reno, Nevada

This book was published with generous financial support obtained
by the Association of Friends of the Center for Basque Studies
from the Provincial Government of Bizkaia.

Basque Classics Series, No. 8
Series Editors: William A. Douglass, Gregorio Monreal, and Pello Salaburu

Center for Basque Studies
University of Nevada, Reno
Reno, Nevada 89557
http://basque.unr.edu

Cover and series design © 2012 by Jose Luis Agote
Cover illustration: Colored illustration from original edition
Portions of this book are reprinted from *Linguae Vasconum Primitiae*.
Bilbao: Euskaltzaindia, 1995. Used by permission.

Library of Congress Cataloging-in-Publication Data

Dechepare, Bernat.
Linguae Vasconum Primitiae : The first fruits of the Basque language, 1545
/ Bernard Etxepare ; Foreword by Pello Salaburu ; Preface by Paxti Altuna ;
Introduction by Beñat Oyharabal ; Translated by Mikel Morris Pagoeta.
    pages cm. -- (Basque Classics Series ; No. 8)
Original Basque with English translation.
Includes bibliographical references and index.
Summary: "Modern translation and original Basque version of the first
book printed in the Basque language in Baiona in 1545"--Provided by
publisher.
ISBN 978-1-935709-32-9 (pbk. : alk. paper) -- ISBN 978-1-935709-33-6
(cloth : alk. paper)
I. Dechepare, Bernat Linguae vasconum primitiae. II. Dechepare, Bernat
Linguae vasconum primitiae. English. III. Title. IV. Title: First fruits of the
Basque language, 1545.

PH5339.D4L513 2013
899'.921--DC23

2012046027

Contents

Foreword: Extepare in the Street

The year 1995 marked the 450th anniversary of the publication in Burgo of *Linguæ Vasconum Primitiæ*, written by Bernard Etxepare, parish priest of the church of Saint-Michel-le-Vieux, in Eyheralarre, a hamlet nearby Donibane Garazi (Saint-Jean-Pied-de-Port), in Lower Navarre. Juan Huarte San Juan, author of *Examen de ingenios para las ciencias* (Examination of the wits for the sciences), was at this time a fifteen-year-old teenager in this pretty little medieval village situated at the foot of the French Pyrenees, on the famous Camino de Santiago.

At the University of the Basque Country we wanted to take advantage of this date to reedit Extepare's book in various languages in addition to its original Basque. Therefore we published a volume in Spanish, English, French, German, and Italian. Etxepare's work had a great deal of symbolic value for the Basques: this is the first book published in the Basque language. As can be observed, it is a fairly small book, written in the Lower Navarrese dialect, that has an author's prologue and fifteen verse compositions on various subjects: religion, love, autobiography—in which the author narrates his experience in the prison at Bearn, where he was imprisoned on charges of treason—and praise of the Basque language. The last two compositions refer precisely to the Basque language; Etxepare was fully conscious of being the author of the first book to be printed in this language. He couldn't have imagined, however, that centuries later his second-to-last composition ("Kontrapas") would end up becoming one of the most popular songs in the Basque language, since it was put to music by the also-poet and singer Xabier Lete (1944–2010) in the 1970s. The verses of this composition were an identity marker for those who reclaimed the language's presence in all social spheres. It was a song that was taught in all of the *Euskaltegis*[1] to the students who were getting to know the language, and it was sung with much pleasure, even

1. *Euskaltegis* are schools that teach the Basque language.

if some of the words escaped the comprehension of the improvised sing-
ers. But the message was very clear, that it was necessary to use the language in all spheres: "*Euskara, jalgi hadi dantzara!*" ("Basque, go forth
and dance!")

The 1995 edition to which constant reference is made in this edition was driven by the vice president of the Basque language's office of
the University of the Basque Country, but other institutions also took
up to the proposal: the University of Deusto, the Public University of
Navarre, with its campus in Iruña-Pamplona, and the government of
Navarre. These institutions financed the edition that was published
under the rubric of Euskaltzaindia, or the Royal Academy of the Basque
Language.

Here we have wanted to take advantage of that material and to complete it. We have used the English version translated by Mikel Morris for
the body of the work. We have also included the original introduction
by Patxi Altuna (1927–2006), one of the greatest scholars fo Etxepare's
work, which was the subject of his doctoral thesis under the direction
of Koldo Mitxelena. In this new edition we have included another introductory study done by Beñat Oyharçabal. Altuna was a professor at the
University of Deusto and member of Euskaltzaindia. Oyharçabal is a
researcher at the National Center for Scientific Research (CNRS by its
French acronym). I mention this information because they relate to two
great masters of knowledge regarding the opus of Etxepare, Basque
researchers who pertain to two generations, two countries, and who have
two very different life trajectories (Jesuit the first, lay person the second).
For this reason they entail two perspectives that complement each other
and that enrich the book's contents.

Nearly half of a millennium has passed for this work, written in
a dialect used by only a few thousand people, and that forms part of
a minority language that barely counts six hundred thousand speakers
(who in addition also speak Spanish or French), now coming to light in
another country, thousands of miles distant that serves as the reference
for the academic world. Thus is completed, once again, Etxepare's desire:
"Euskera, jalgi hadi plazara!" (Basque, go forth into the street!").

— Pello Salaburu

*Professor of Basque linguistics at the University of
the Basque Country, member of Euskaltzaindia,
and coeditor of the Basque Classics Series.*

Preface to the 1995 Edition

"In reality the relationship of Etxepare's work with folk poetry—
in spirit, language, and versification —is readily apparent."

— Luis Michelena, *Historia de la literatura Vasca*

The 450th anniversary of the publication by Bernard Etxepare of the
first known Basque book in print—*Linguæ Vasconum Primitiæ,* 1545
in Bordeaux—is an important enough day in the annals of the Basque
language and culture not to go unnoticed by the institutions, universities,
and cultural entities of the country without properly paying homage to
his memory. Nothing seemed more fitting than a re-edited facsimile of
his work accompanied by a translation into the most widespread languages of the Western world so as to fulfill the desire which the poet had
expressed: "*Zeren ladin publika mundu guzietara berze lengoaiak bezala
hain eskribatzeko on dela*" (so that the whole world might know that it
is as good as any tongue in which to write).

Scholars of the history of the language are not unanimous in regarding the poet's rightful place. Koldo Mitxelena differs not only from those
who call him "the Basque Rabelais," but also from those who call him a
Renaissance man. In his opinion, the poet is worthy of the name merely
on account of his enthusiasm for the printed word. He agrees, on the
other hand, with the age-old parallelism established between him and
the Archpriest of Hita, and argues that some passages he does not believe
were composed by Etxepare.[1] Jon Juaristi believes him to be a "transi-
tory figure between medieval and Renaissance culture."[2]

In our day and age a possible connection has been revealed between
the Basque poet and the famous French poet Clément Marot (1497—

---

1. Michelena, *Historia de la literatura Vasca*, 46.
2. Jon Juaristi, *Literatura Vasca* (Madrid: Ed. Taurus, 1987), 33.

1544), the favorite of Marguerite, the Queen of Navarre who were brought together, on account of a common friendship, by the King's counsel Bernard Lehete, patron and receiver of Etxepare's work and protector of Marot in difficult situations, whose work might have been known by Etxepare through their common friend.

There is no common agreement among critics either when judging the poetic value of Etxepare's work. While Julio de Urquijo and, above all, Schuchardt, believe he hardly possesses the qualities of a true poet, Mrs. Gil Reicher and Mitxelena believe otherwise. The former writes, "Ces poésies sont empreinte d'une lyrisme, d'une passion, d'une force, que l'eskuara retrouvera rarement. Et je ne crois pas que ce soit un paradoxe de dire que notre premier poète basque peut-être le plus grand." (These poems are imprints of lyricism, of passion, of a vitality which Basque rarely finds. And I do not believe it to be a paradox to say that the first Basque poet of ours may be the greatest).[3]

As for Mitxelena, after stating that being a poet does not involve choosing this or that poetic metre, and whatever is chosen, it is necessary to soar, "To rise to a plane which is found situated where no one knows nor by whom" and that whoever fails to scale this height does not deserve to be called a poet, he further adds: "Nik uste dut, eta zenbat ere gehiago irakutzen dudan are sengoago uste dut, gure Etxepare igo zela, zegokion neurrian eta begiz jo zuen bidez, diodan maila horretara eta iritzi hori berori dute oraingo gehienek." (I believe, and the more I read him the more I am convinced of it, that our Etxepare rose, as far as he could up the path he blazed, to the level I am talking about and most are of the very same opinion).[4]

Born in Donibane Garazi or thereabouts, Etxepare availed himself of his Eastern Lower Navarrese dialect in the very same way that the people used it without as much as modifying any of its phonetic characteristics in a certain refined, yet to be standardized language. "Nor should," wrote Mitxelena, "the common character, as it were, of Etxepare's language be forgotten."[5]

---

3. Gil Reicher, *St.-Jean-Pied-de-Port en Navarre, Bordeaux*, (N.p.: Delmas, 1938), 28.

4. Koldo Mitxelena, "Sarrera gisa," in *Mitxelenaren Euskal Idazlan Guztiak V*, no. 25 (Donostia-San Sebastián: Euskal Editoreen Elkartea, 1988), 28.

5. Koldo Mitxelena, "Prólogo" in Patxi Altuna, *Versificación de Dechepare: Métrica y pronunciación* (Bilbao: Ed. Mensajero, 1979), 9.

His work covers compositions which, on account of their content, are usually divided into four parts: two of a religious theme, ten dealing with romantic subjects, one which intones freedom and the last two which wax lyrically over Basque. There are those, such as Lafon, who think that there could have been a previous edition which was smaller and entirely lost: the fact that there is doubling of consonants, among other indicators, found in some odd compositions leads one to think that it can only be attributable to two different periods. Where there is no doubt is the existence of a previous one, only known since Pierre Lafitte published in 1967 a little work by the hitherto unknown Arnaud Oihenarte (1665) in which the Zuberoa poet speaks of a second (but quite incorrect) edition which appeared in Pau a hundred years after the first one.[6]

The work does not seem to have been widely diffused judging by the fact that only a single copy has survived to this day without our knowing about the work and about which posterior authors, such as Pouvreau, were ignorant—though Oihenarte was not—not only of the first but also of the second edition as stated above. Isasti's testimony (1625), however, failed to transcend on account of the failure to publish his *Compendia* until 1850. It is surprising that Larramendi did not know about it judging by the omission of it in his account of previous writers whom he inserted in his Dictionary (1745). In the account where Joannes Leizarraga takes up all of chapter 20 after a description of a dozen printed Basque books he says to have been acquainted with, Etxepare is conspicuous by his absence.[7] Even more so if one bears in mind the fact that Etxeberri de Sara, at that time a doctor in Azkoitia, had many an opportunity to let the Jesuit from Loyola know about him. Or else could it be that the writer from Sara was also unaware of his existence?

If its initial diffusion was scant, the same cannot be said for its diffusion in the centuries which followed. In 1847, Francisque Michel informed Mr. Brunet about the existence of an old Basque book in the National Library in Paris which he thought worthy of being printed and which was published in the journal *Acte de l'Academie Royale des Sciences* with Jean B. Archu's French translation. It is also ridden with errors if we are to believe Vinson who was moved to come out with a new edition with Hovelacque's help. Nevertheless, despite his pretension of it

---

6. Arnaud Oihenart, "L'Art Poetique Basque," in *Gure Herria* (Baiona, 1967), 227.

7. Manuel Larramendi, *Diccionario Trilingüe* (Donostia: 1745), 36.

being "absolument conforme à la première de 1545" (steadfastly true to the original 1545 version), it too failed to be free of numerous errata.

The research done on Etxepare's work up to then which deserves special mention is the outstanding work of the German linguist Victor Stempf, who in addition to the other 1893 edition—the best one of all to date—prepared a complete glossary of all the words appearing in Etxepare's work with a complete description of each. If we reckon in, along with four further editions in our century, including the 1995 edition—the first and finest of them which Urquijo published as a facsimile in the RIEV (*Revista Internacional de Estudios Vascos*) in 1933 the painstaking work of illustrious linguists such as Schuchardt, Ernst Lewy, and especially René Lafon, who were singularly attracted by the archaic nature of his language and who zealously researched it, we can safely state without fear of contradiction that philological and linguistic knowledge of the work in question hardly poses any mystery for today's linguists.

Nevertheless, the same could not be said for the state of literary research done on the work as none of the linguists above, with the exception of Lafon, paid any attention whatsoever to the poetry hidden behind the language and to this day no one has seriously taken on the task so that, once and for all, there would be no doubt as to whether or not he deserves his place among the greatest poets. However, only a Basque-speaker who has learnt the language at his mother's lap could carry out this task as no other could hardly appreciate the precious jewels contained in the work as Van Eys aptly pointed out; "Pour ce qui regarde la valeur poétique des poésies de Dechepare, nous la laisserons à l'appreciation des Basques eux-mêmes" (As for the poetic value of Etxepare's poetry, we should leave it to the Basques themselves) and precisely because he, not being a Basque-speaker himself, dared to make a value judgment or two, made the mistake of disparaging its inherent beauty, and hurled broadsides of this nature: "On debra admettre, qu'il y a beaucoup de ses poésies qui ne sont ni élevées comme pensée ni correctes grammaticalement" (it should be admitted that there is a great deal of his poetry which is neither elevated in thought nor grammatically correct).[8]

The poet whose work is the first one in the Basque language, seems, as stated above, to have nevertheless been profoundly inspired by the

---

8. W. Van Eys, "Le Dialecte de Dechepare" in *Euskara: Organ für die Interessen der Baskischen Gesellschaft*, no. 1 (Berlin, 1886), 2.

popular religious tradition as demonstrated by the fact that Resurrección María de Azkue took down some verses from the lips of the people in Zaraitzu (Salazar) Valley, as did Father Donostia in Otxagabia, which had been conserved in the folk memory for perhaps centuries and are quite similar to some passages by the Basque poet or, rather, his are quite similar to latter, from which he undoubtedly gained inspiration.

Nevertheless, the poet is clearly conscious of offering an authentic "primitia" or first fruit, as indicated in the title of the book *Linguæ Vasconum Primitiæ* as no one before him had composed or at least printed a book in the Basque language which, far from giving him a feeling of pride, left him feeling rather amazed (*miraz nago*) in observing that while no Basque, in spite of the fact that there were among them not a few "skilled, hard-working and genteel" ones, had previously tried to show the world that the Basque language was "as good as any tongue to write in" and at the same time he had a certain hope that "upcoming generations might be motivated to perfect it," for which he did not balk at crying "Heuſcara ialgui adi dançara," (Basque, go forth and dance).

Mitxelena was able like no other to sense and express this happy and delightful entry of the Basque language onto the literary stage when he wrote, "few languages have made as joyful an entry into literature as Basque did when the poet Etxepare called for it to dance. This . . . made it greater and he was fully aware that he was doing something greater for, in other words, he was the first to introduce Basque onto the world stage. When he ended his verses by writing "*debile principium melior fortuna sequatum*" (out of a humble beginning may better fortune follow), he undoubtedly believed that he was laying the first milestone which would mark the way down through the centuries.[9]

There has been a great deal of speculation from Prince Lucien Bonaparte's day down to the present regarding the archaic nature of Etxepare's language viz-á-viz Joannes Leizarraga's or, if you prefer, vice versa. Of course, Mitxelena never made comparisons between the two and spoke in no uncertain terms about the archaic nature of Leizarraga. However, he seems to be inclined to follow the view of Prince Bonaparte's that there is a greater degree of archaism in the language of the trans-

---

9. Koldo Mitxelena, "Euskal literaturaren etorkizuna," in *Mitxelenaren Euskal Idazlan Guztiak IV*, no. 24, (Donostia-San Sebastián: Euskal Editoreen Elkartea, 1988), 24.

lator's *Testamentu Berria* (New Testament) when he, in our opinion, quotes a questionable reference from a passage by Schuchardt.[10]

In effect, when the latter states that Leizarraga's language is no less odd for the Basque of his age than Luther's German was for his contemporary Germans—something which is so plainly obvious that he might have meant something else since Luther and Leizarraga were almost contemporaries who were separated by only fifty years—by this he does not intend, in our opinion, to play up the archaic nature of Leizarraga's language as opposed to Etxepare's but rather, he simply seeks to excuse himself, as it were, from offering the new edition of the *Testamentu Berria* which he prepared, in contemporary speech and spelling to the taste of the modern reader and in the same way as Inchauspe had done some years back with Axular's *Gero*. He reproduces, on the other hand, the original text just as it appeared in the first edition which he points out as proof positive of the archaic nature of Leizarraga's language in the same way that Luther's is less susceptible to modifications than Axular's, which is why it never occurred to anyone to re-edit the German theologian with changes in his language and spelling.[11]

Whatever the reason, Lafon is adamant when, after discussing Prince Bonaparte's reasons, he concludes: "Etxepare is as archaic, if not more so, than Leizarraga and his language is much more coherent. Even if we have nothing else to go on except *Linguæ Vasconum Primitiæ* one can get a precise and reliable idea, thanks to Etxepare, of the Basque linguistic structure in the sixteenth century."[12]

Now for a few words about Etxepare's metrics in conclusion. Lafon rightfully claims that Basque metrics stem from medieval Latin poetry.[13] Except for four of the fifteen parts comprising the work, the rest correspond to the same pattern that every scholar of Basque metrics, including Oihenarte, had unanimously defined as a compound of hemistichs with obligatory caesura of eight and seven syllables respectively. Let us not

---

10. Luis Michelena, *Historia de la Literatura Vasca* (Madrid: Ed. Minotauro, 1960), 50.

11. Hugo Schuchardt, *Uber die Einrichtung des Neudrucks: Insbesondere über die Druck-fehler und Varianten bei Leizarraga* (in German), 134 (in Spanish), in *I. Leiça-rragas Baskische Bücher von 1571* (Bilbao: Euskaltzaindia, 1990).

12. Rene Lafon, *Le Systeme du Verbe Basque Au Siècle*, (Donostia: Ed. Elkar, 1980), 48.

13. René Lafon, "Sur la versification de Dechepare," *Boletín de la Real Sociedad Vascongada de los amigos del país* (1957): 392.

forget religious hymns such as *"Tantum ergo sacramentum veneremur cernuh."* It was Mitxelena who was first to take note of the existence of strong secondary traits in each one of both hemistichs in which the verse pattern of Etxepare's is 4/4//4/3. Against hitherto prevalent conventional wisdom, Jon Juaristi has defended the theory that Etxepare's verses are parallel with the ballad genre and comes to the conclusion that, erroneous in our opinion, the verses in question have sixteen syllables as the last one is oxytone.[14]

Try as he might, Oihenarte was wrong to say that the fifteen-syllable verse was previously unknown, even in Latin poetry.[15] Verses such as *"Tantum vini habet nemo quantum fudit sanguinis"* (third century) and those from an ecclesiastical hymn which goes *"Apparebit repentina dies magna Domini"* and stanzas from the consecration of the Milan cathedral in 738 which begins *"Rerum cernitur cunctarum inclita speciebus."* Here we are unable to point out, however superficially, the characteristics of this versification which, except for its written character, fully coincides with *bertsolarismo*[16] which, nevertheless, has its own equivalent in the form of *bertso paperak*.[17]

If expressing a wish is in order, may this homage serve to inspire some of our young graduates of Basque philology to fill the yawning gap in literary analysis of Etxepare's work and find in it the distinguished popular poet who sprinkled his work with sayings and proverbs.

— Patxi Altuna

---

14. Jon Juaristi, *Arte en el País Vasco* (Madrid: Ed. Cátedra, 1987), 127.

15. Arnaud Oihenart, "L'Art Poetique Basque," in *Gure Herria* (Baiona, 1967), 205–29.

16. Genre of Basque folk poetry based on improvization and performed by *bertsolaris*, who, like troubadours or bards, perform in groups in various public places. The meter and rhythm of their verses are based on various traditional tunes.

17. (Lit. 'verse papers') The *bertsolaris'* compositions appeared on these printed sheets of paper. They often contained more elaborate poetry while still following the formal rules of the genre. They were sold during fairs and festivals and touched on subjects of current and local interest.

Bibliography

Juaristi, Jon. *Arte en el País Vasco*. Madrid: Catedra, 1987.

———. *Literatura Vasca*. Madrid: Ed. Taurus, 1987.

Lafon, René. "Sur la versification de Dechepare." *Boletín de la Real Sociedad Vascongada de los amigos del país* (1957): 387-93.

———. *Le systeme du verbe Basque au siècle*. Donostia-San Sebastián: Elkar, 1980.

Larramendi, Manuel. *Diccionario Trilingüe*. Donostia, 1745.

Mitxelena, Koldo. "Euskal literaturaren etorkizuna" in *Mitxelenaren Euskal Idazlan Guztiak IV*, no. 24. Donostia-San Sebastián: Euskal Editoreen Elkartea, 1988.

——— [Michelena, Luis]. *Historia de la literatura Vasca*. Madrid: Ed. Minotauro, 1960.

———. "Prologo." In *Versificacion de Dechepare: Metrica y pronunciation*. Bilbao: Ed. Mensajero, 1979.

———. "Sarrera gisa" in *Mitxelenaren Euskal Idazlan Guztiak V*, no. 25. Donostia-San Sebastián: Euskal Editoreen Elkartea, 1988.

Oihenart, Arnaud. "L'Art Poetique Basque." *Gure Herria* 4 (1967): 205–229.

Reicher, Gil. *St.-Jean-Pied-de-Port en Navarre, Bordeaux*. N.p.: Ed. Delmas, 1938.

Schuchardt, Hugo. *Uber die Einrichtung des Neudrucks: Insbesondere über die Druck-fehler und Varianten bei Leigarraga*. Bilbao: Euskaltzaindia, 1990.

Van Eys, W. "Le Dialecte de Dechepare." In *Euskara: Organ fur die Interessen der Baskischen Gesellschaft*. Berlin, 1886.

A Note on Literary Historiography: Bernard Etxepare, a Medieval Author?

Beñat Oyharçabal

Just as a curious observer of the field, I venture here to make some observations on several old issues concerning the historiography of Basque literature, hoping, at the same time, that literary history scholars will not take exception to this and will excuse my daring. The article is intended to be a survey of a paradox I have long wished to address: there have been very few exceptions to the often mentioned late development of Basque literature from 1545 until the rich legacy of the last century, and one of them, in my opinion, is Etxepare's *Linguæ Vasconum Primitiæ*. In general, Basque literature has been old-fashioned and outdated, but Etxepare's book of stanzas is a clear exception to that (as are Joannes Leizarraga's translations, although outside the field of literary creation), and cannot be taken to be the beginning of a chronic delay. At the same time, one only has to look back over the last five decades to realize that many scholars of the history of Basque literature have argued in the opposite direction: in fact, what is been argued is that Etxepare was a precursor and a symbol of that out-of-date literature and, furthermore, that he was a medieval author. My first goal here is to explore when, how, and by whom this idea was brought up, spread, and established, and at the same time, to discuss arguments and viewpoints that were proposed in order to support that idea, or that emerged as a consequence of it. In particular, I will confront the idea that Etxepare was an uneducated poet, something akin to a *bertsolari* ("improvisational poet") of the new era.

---

* Originally published as "Ohar bat literatura historiografiaz: B. Echepare Erdi-Aroko autore?" in various authors, *Jean Haritschelhar-i omenaldia: Homenaje a Jean Haritschelhar; Hommage a Jean Haritschelhar.* Iker 21 (Bilbao: Euskaltzaindia, 2008), 119–49. Translated by Aritz Branton.

The Similarity between Etxepare's and Ruiz's Work (Proposed by Etxaide) and the Medieval Nature of Etxepare's Work (Defended by Mitxelena)

As we know, the history of Basque literature and Basque texts, as well as the studies about the Basque language, owe an immense amount to Koldo Mitxelena, the promoter and disseminator of modern Basque linguistics and philology in the second half of the twentieth century. So, it comes as no surprise that Mitxelena established many of the main ideas about the first Basque author.

In his *Historia de la literatura vasca* (The History of Basque Literature, 1960), Mitxelena clearly states that Etxepare was a medieval author and not, except for his attitude to printing and his defense of the Basque language, a man of the Renaissance:[1]

> When Francisque-Michel and Vinson called him "the Basque Rabelais," they were far from the truth. The comparison is inappropriate not only because Etxepare was not a prose writer, but also because there is nothing in his work, except his enthusiasm for printing (which he hoped—if we are to take his words literally—would raise Basque above all other languages) that marks him as a Renaissance man. Above all, he was a medieval author.[2]

It was the first time that this point, that is the medieval nature of Etxepare's work, had been emphasized in such a way in Basque literature.[3] Let's inquire into the arguments that Mitxelena gave for focusing his research in this direction. Unfortunately, as he only wrote very few lines about this subject in his book, there is no exact explanation for Mitxel-

---

1. In fact, Mitxelena had already expressed this idea in 1958, in an essay published in Guillermo Díaz Plaja, ed., *Historia general de las literaturas hispánicas*, vol. 5 (Barcelona: Barna, 1958), 341–86. The lines about Etxepare that Mitxelena includes in his 1960 book are taken from this previous essay.

2. Luis Michelena [Koldo Mitxelena], *Historia de la literatura vasca* (Madrid: Minotauro, 1960), 46-47.

3. In the Southern Basque Country too, authors who wrote before the Spanish Civil War classified Etxepare as a Renaissance writer. Aitzol (José Ariztimuño), for example, called Etxepare the first Renaissance Basque after comparing him to several other sixteenth-century Navarrese authors who had chosen to write in Spanish (Pedro Malón de Echaide and Diego de Estella, in particular). See José Ariztimuño, "El primer renacentista y poeta euskeldun" *Yakintza* 1 (1933): 12–20.

ena's opinion, and, as far as I know, he never mentioned this idea again in his work.[4]

As can be seen in the above quote, while Francisque Michel and Julien Vinson compared Etxepare with Rabelais, Mitxelena argued against this idea, comparing him to an author from another age, Juan Ruiz, who had written two centuries before Etxepare and had combined religious and amorous subject matters in his writing: "The similarity with Juan Ruiz is obvious. And the reason for this is not only that they were both priests, but also that they both combine religious and erotic subject matter in their work, dealing with them in a very relaxed fashion."[5] In this quote, it is clear that the main influence on Mitxelena's attitude toward Etxepare was his outright, unembarrassed combination of religious and amorous subject matter in his stanzas, something similar to what is found in the Archpriest of Hita's verses. This seems to be the only argument Mitxelena had in mind.

Due to the fact that Mitxelena mentioned more than once the old-fashioned poetic tradition of Etxepare, perhaps one could ask whether Mitxelena had not taken his poetic forms into account when classifying him as an author from a previous era. For instance, Patxi Salaberri Muñoa writes about the medieval nature of his stanza's formal parameters.[6] However, the main meter (8+7) and rhyming technique (assonance) that Etxepare used can hardly be considered to have been an anachronism in Basque stanzas of the time, because they were predominant in the poetry of sixteenth- and seventeenth-century books, at least in the Northern Basque Country.[7] In fact, the meter (8+7) was extremely widespread at that time, as Arnaud Oihenart pointed out in 1665 when mentioning Etxepare, Etxegaray, Logras, and Etxeberri, and as Mitxelena himself shows in the context of seventeenth-century Lapurdi poets' work (Etxeberri, Harizmendi, and Argaignaratz).[8] Although I do accept that the

---

4. For example, the introduction to the 1968 publication of *Linguæ Vasconum Primitiæ* said nothing about the medieval nature of Etxepare's work, nor did it compare him with Juan Ruiz.

5. Michelena, *Historia de la literatura vasca*, 47.

6. "His written work followed the formal parameters of the Middle Ages," Patxi Salaberri Muñoa, *Iraupena eta lekukotasuna: Euskal literatura idatzia 1900 arte* (Donostia: Elkar, 2002), 60.

7. I have not analyzed Lazarraga's poetry in depth, but I have not found stanzas with that meter among them.

8. See Arnaud Oihenart, *Art poétique basque* (1665; rpt., suppl. in *Gure Herria* 1967) and Michelena, *Historia de la literatura vasca*, 66.

meters and rhyming techniques of those stanzas are also to be found in a previous tradition,[9] the usual composition of these stanzas cannot be an appropriate criteria in itself for placing a poet of the sixteenth or seventeenth century in an era he did not live in, and furthermore, classify him as a poet of the late Middle Ages. Mitxelena's arguments are mainly based on the contents of the stanzas, and not on their form. I will return to this issue later on.

From Moral Arguments to Arguments about Literary History

As Eduardo Gil Bera points out, Mitxelena was not the first one to compare Etxepare to Ruiz in Basque literary historiography.[10] In fact, Yon Etxaide had used the same argument a little earlier, precisely in his book *Amasei seme Euskalerriko* (Sixteen Sons from the Basque Country).[11] Etxaide's work—which was awarded a prize by the Academy of the Basque Language—had been published two years earlier with a foreword by Mitxelena.

However, while Mitxelena agreed with Etxaide in emphasizing the similarity of the combination of subject matters in both Ruiz's and Etxepare's work, their motivation to reach this conclusion was completely different. As a student of Basque literary history, Mitxelena wanted to explain the literary influences in Etxepare's stanzas, and, to do so, he dealt with the place given to the various subject matters and the use made of them. Etxaide, on the other hand, seeking to inform Basques about their own literature, did not want that the Church judged the risky writing of the priest Etxepare as a moral offense or that his writing was taken as anachronical: "At that time, it was common for priests and friars to write lascivious texts. In support of my words, I will only mention what the famous Spanish historian Rafael Altamira says about Juan Ruiz, the Archpriest of Hita, as an example of the way of life of those times."[12]

---

9. See Luis Michelena, "Sarrera gisa," (intro) in Bernard Dechepare, *Olerkiak: 1545* (Donostia-San Sebastián: Edili, 1968) and Patxi Altuna, "Etxepare, herri poeta," in various authors, *Euskal linguistika eta literatura: Bide berriak* (Bilbao: Deustuko Unibertsitatea, 1981).

10. Eduardo Gil Bera, "Melior fortuna," *Mazantini* 2 (1992). Available on the Armiarma website at http://andima.armiarma.com/maza/maza0208.htm.

11. Jon Etxaide, *Amasei seme Euskalerriko*, Kuliska sorta 21–22 (Zarautz: Itxaropena, 1958).

12. Ibid., 68.

Etxaide then quotes extensively the book *Historia de España y de la civilización española* (History of Spain and Spanish Civilization) by the historian Altamira,[13] with the objective of showing that, with regard to Christian morality, the behavior of Churchmen in previous centuries should not be judged using the standards that were established in a later period: "At first, we are startled by Juan Ruiz's lack of morality and by an apparent mixing up of devotion to God, moral teachings, and cynicism. But this confusion should not overly concern us, as this was a characteristic of the poetry of the time, as we will see later. On the other hand, the nature of the writer was also like that, he enjoyed a debauched life, as members of the clergy of the time often did."[14]

Bearing in mind the influence that the Church and its moral doctrine had on scholars of Basque letters at previous times, it comes as no surprise that Etxaide used such apologetic arguments to defend Etxepare's poetry. Etxaide combined his enthusiasm for Basque culture with typical Christian values, which became inseparable in his life as well as in his work. One should also bear in mind that Basque culture was still highly restricted in those very difficult years of the 1950s, and when literary subject matters were mentioned and Basque authors introduced, it was hard for Etxaide to simply condemn the first Basque writer's poetry as his Christian conscience would have compelled him to do.[15] In that sense it was helpful for him to compare Etxepare with Ruiz, who enjoyed some status in the Spanish literature. Ruiz had also been a priest and had also dealt very freely with both religious and amorous subject matter –making use of his own experience, according to Altamira and Etxaide. As in the case of Ruiz, who was the author of *El libro de buen amor* (The Book of Good Love), Etxaide requested that the same relativism be used to judge Etxepare. There is no doubt that Etxaide compared Etxepare

---

13. See Rafael Altamira, *Historia de España y de la civilización española*, foreword J. M. Jover (1900–1911; 4th ed., rpt., Barcelona: Crítica, 2001), vol. 1, 570, 529.

14. Rafael Altamira, quoted by Etxaide, *Amasei seme Euskalerriko*, 69.

15. At first, Orixe (Nicolás Ormaechea) took a different approach, particularly dealing with Etxepare's religious subject matter, and almost silenced his amorous subject matter, hardly mentioning it in fact. This is all he says about it: "In the first verses about love, these two lines are to be found: Some people had something else in mind / I was thinking of the Virgin Mother [in other words, he included the love poems in the poems in homage to the Virgin Mother]. Apart from that, there are some fairly crude things in the love verses. In this respect, the heart can be a great help; it seems this subject matter was very common at the time." See Orixe, *Euskal literaturaren historia laburra* (1927; rpt., ed. Paulo Iztueta, Donostia: Utriusque Vasconiæ, 2002), 38.

with Ruiz for moral reasons, without taking literary considerations into account, considering specially the *excessively relaxed lifestyles* of the two writers.

In the 1950s, the mentality that influenced Etxaide adopt this attitude was widespread among Basque writers, an attitute that had been equally prevalent during the previous three centuries. The observations by Oihenart, Jean-Baptiste Archu, and Pierre Lafitte in, the seventeenth, nineteenth, and twentieth centuries respectively, were well known and have often been quoted.[16] The illustrious scholar Luis Villasante also took the same route as Etxaide, and used exactly Etxaide's same arguments when discussing the work by Etxepare in his *Historia de la literatura vasca* (The History of Basque Literature); he mentions the Archpriest of Hita in order to underline the similarity between the two authors and also uses the argument of historical relativity for Etxepare's poetry not to be judged as *incorrect* from a Christian point of view.[17]

Even though Mitxelena's and Etxaide's arguments had the same basis, they were completely different in nature, and it goes without saying that Mitxelena in no way aimed to whitewash Etxepare's behavior or the crudeness of his stanzas from the point of view of the Church's moral. It

---

16. Oihenart saw them as "very inappropriate love verses for a Churchman, and even more so for a priest looking after souls," *Art poétique basque*, 37. Archu did not record his thoughts on this, but when Gustave Brunet asked him to translate Etxepare's poems for the 1847 edition he was working on, he refused to translate the last two stanzas and "In Defense of Women" / "Emazten Fabore" into French, perhaps because they embarrassed him (*Linguæ Vasconum Primitiæ*, 3, 55–62). So the book was published without a translation of those verses which sing to the beauty of love, the Basque text having been censured out of the French text. See Francisque Michel, *Le Pays Basque: Sa population, sa langue, ses moeurs, sa littérature et sa musique* (Paris: F. Didot, 1857), 441 and Julien Vinson, *Essai d'une bibliographie de la langue basque* (1891), rpt., foreword by Luis Michelena, 2 vols. (Donostia-San Sebastián: ASJU, Gipuzkoako Foru Aldundia, 1984). Lafitte followed the same way of thinking: "It [Etxepare's book] contains beautiful passages, but, to tell the truth, also many things that a priest, certainly, should not write" Pierre Lafitte, *Eskualdunen loretegia* (Baiona: Lasserre, 1931), 7.

17. "It is true that there are passages of extreme realism in the amourous poems, unimaginable today for a priest to write and, in fact, for any Christian to write. But we may be in danger of being unfair here by judging an author from a period and surroundings very different from our own. It is well known that in recent centuries the Christian social atmosphere, and the literature that reflects it, has been restrained and measured to an extent that was unknown in previous eras. And what today seems scandalous and incomprehensible to us, was not so in the poet's time, or, at least, not so much." Luis Villasante, *Historia de la literatura vasca* (1961; rpt., Oñati: Arantzazu, 1979), 54.

seems, then, that there was something of a misunderstanding due to this comparison. Etxaide, and in general Villasante too, had, in a sense, the diachronic relativism of church morality in mind when they mentioned the Archpriest of Hita. Mitxelena, on the other hand, believed the comparison was appropriate from the point of view of both literary history and the characters of the authors. And as he treated the issue taking into account that point of view, bearing in mind that there was a difference of two centuries between Ruiz and Etxepare, he used the argument to classify Etxepare as a medieval author.

This idea, very successfull at the time, may have emerged from private correspondence or conversation. Bearing in mind the ups and downs of Basque cultural life at the time, that would not have been surprising. In any case, the comparison with Ruiz appeared for the first time in Etxaide's writing, although—and in my opinion there is little doubt about this—it was through Mitxelena that the idea became widespread among literary historians, and, as a result, most literary histories place Etxepare's stanzas in the Middle Ages.

Etxepare, a Precursor and Symbol of Basque Literature's Lateness?

After Mitxelena published the idea that Etxepare was a medieval author, this idea became very widely accepted and it was repeated in most literary history books published in the Southern Basque Country in the following decades. Until recently, very few authors have questioned the medieval nature of Etxepare's work[18]—excluding the subjects of printing and the Basque language—as if it were an extremely self-evident truth. Furthermore, this idea also strengthened another generalization about Basque literature (which is why it became so widespread): the generalization that, from the very beginning, Basque literature is out-of-date and delayed. This generalization is seen as an enduring, innate cause of harm to the development of Basque letters; just like Mitxelena (1960),[19] many other authors have taken it as a given fact. Indeed Ibon Sarasola brought it up ironically: *The Basques are always late!*[20]

---

18. However, see Jon Kortazar, "Bernard d'Etxepare bidegurutzean," *Entseiucarrean* 12 (1996), 29–35 and *Euskal literaturaren historia txikia: Ahozkoa eta klasikoa (XVI–XIX)*, 2nd ed. (Donostia-San Sebastián: Erein, 2000), 85–86.

19. Michelena, *Historia de la literatura vasca*.

20. Ibon Sarasola, "Euskal poesia gaur," *Jakin* 24 (1967): 12–19.

I am not going to discuss at length whether the fact of being delayed has long afflicted Basque literature. What is clear is that Basques, from the sixteenth century to present, have continually been subject to diglossic behavior (in the creative area, among others), subject to difficulties down the centuries to adapt quickly to literary trends and innovations. However, it is by no means clear where the first signs of *achrony* can be found in Etxepare's poetry.[21]

As I noted before, Mitxelena and the literary historians who have followed his line of research have been very clear about the fact that there is a side of Etxepare's work that must be linked with the Renaissance. Indeed, there is a particularly Renaissance flavor in the stanzas that deal with the world of printing in order to praise the Basque language. It would be hard to refute that the Etxepare who dealt with that subject shows a warm-hearted optimism that is tightly connected with the ideas and the literature of that time.[22] After Mitxelena's writing on the subject, Etxepare's championing of the Basque language was not taken seriously (which, on the other hand, was a very important matter for him, as can be seen in his dedication), and it was dealt with as if it were a matter of secondary importance.

Thus, considering the stanzas that do not deal with the subject of printing, Etxepare has become a symbol of Basque literature's tardiness, as if his writing were a late ripening fruit of the Middle Ages, written after its own time. According to Sarasola, for example, "Etxepare is a late writer of medieval poetry."[23] Taking the paradox to its extreme, while dealing with the work of an author who proudly held himself to be a precursor of Basque literature and a path opener, Sarasola continues: "He *closed* a period in Basque literature," and Etxepare's archaism is also mentioned.[24] Jon Juaristi follows the same line of argumentation

---

21. "His [Etxepare's] work . . . anticipates an *achrony* that was to be endemic in Basque literature in the following centuries," Jon Juaristi, *Literatura vasca* (Madrid: Taurus, 1987), 37.

22. Jean Haritschelhar, "Défense et illustration de la langue basque au XVIe siècle: La *Sautrela* de Bernat Echepare," in *Hommage à Jacques Allières: I. Domaine basque et pyrénéen*, ed. Michel Aurnague and Michel Roché Anglet (Biarritz: Atlantica, 2002), 119–27.

23. Ibon Sarasola, *Historia de la literatura vasca* (Madrid: Akal, 1976), 37.

24. Ibid., 39 (emphasis added).

and confirms: "Etxepare is, in fact, a *primitive* writer." On the other hand, Gorka Aulestia describes him as a *late medieval*.[25]

The comparison Mitxelena made between Etxepare and Ruiz was not questioned by any work on Basque literature published from the 1970s to the 1990s. In fact, after praising the poems about the sacred love of God and physical love between men and women by two poets, Juaristi believes to have found another point in common between them; specifically, he believes that Etxepare, by asking to improve his work (as Ruiz had done before), showed that he had not really understood the world of the age of printing, as if for him texts were still changeable as they had been in previous eras:

> The Navarrese poet states at the end of the dedication that he would accept his potential readers to perfect the doctrine and the subject matter of his book. . . . Etxepare does not seem to be aware of the radical difference between oral works—"open" by definition, subject to change when they are reproduced . . . and works "closed" to all change. . . . Etxepare is a transitional writer . . . between an age in which the oral tradition was preeminent and the new world of printing.[26]

This is a highly questionable interpretation. It was quite common among the writers of the time, when talking about their own work, to express the hope that others would later write better works (and this can, on occasion, be a challenge); this was the case before printing was invented, and continues to be so afterward too. It is very difficult to argue on this basis that a sixteenth-century author spoke in such a way due to the fact that his view of literature was limited to oral literature; even less so in this case: as Etxepare was the first person to have a book printed in Basque, it comes as no surprise that he used this common saying. In fact, this same quote in Latin can be found in the last words of the book by

---

25. Juaristi, *Literatura vasca*, 37; Aulestia, "Bernat Dechepare—Medieval or Renaissance Writer?" in *The Basque Poetic Tradition* (Reno: University of Nevada Press, 2000), 52–60. Translation by Linda White of "Bernat Dechepare, escritor medieval o renacentista?" *Muga* 78 (1991): 86–93. Aulestia, unlike Sarasola and Juaristi, underscores the weakness of the comparison with Ruiz. However, he does support the idea that Etxepare was a medieval writer and emphasizes the paradox still more by seeing Ruiz as an early precursor or remote pioneer of the Renaissance and Etxepare, who was writing two centuries later, as a late medieval writer.

26. Juaristi, *Literatura vasca*, 33.

Ovid, which would also points in the same direction.[27] There was no connection between that and the influence of an oral tradition, which would have brought openness to text modification. There is no doubt that Etxepare was encouraging the writers that would follow to extend the path he opened, writing richer, better works and improving on the stanzas he had written.[28] In the following century, Joanes Etxeberri from Ziburu expressed the same wish to the "devoted readers" of his *Manual Debozionezkoa* (Devotional Handbook).[29]

Hasteak gaitzak direla errana duk komunki
Hunen gañean egiñen dik zenbait berzek hobeki

It is commonly said that starting things is difficult
And that others should go on and do better things

In the same way, it seems to me that taking Etxepare's optimism about the importance of printing for the Basque language as a sign of a

---

27. Etxepare did not mention the author of the quote (*Debile principium melior fortuna sequatur*) and we do not know exactly where it comes from. In his critical edition, Patxi Altuna states that "it seems to be from Ovid," Bernard Echepare, *Linguæ Vasconum Primitiæ*, ed. Patxi Altuna (1545; rpt., Bilbao: Euskaltzaindia and Mensajero, 1980), 261. Although that may be indirectly true, Etxepare almost certainly did not take it from Ovid's writing in itself, because Ovid wrote the same sentence in a slightly different way: *Flebile principium melior fortuna secuta est* (*Metamorphoses*, book 7, 518). Rabelais too (although in a very different context) used the quote in the same form as Etxepare (in some editions, at least, with a change of verb form): *Debile principium melior fortuna sequetur* (book 3, chapter 42). This does not mean that Etxepare took his quote from Rabelais's work, because the book 3 (*Tiers livre*) was published in 1546. However, it must have been a well known quote that had long been included in books of sayings and proverbs.

28. See also Patxi Altuna, "Son hexadecasílabicos los versos de Dechepare?" in *Memoriæ Mitxelena Magistri Sacrum*, ed. Joseba Lakarra and Iñigo Ruiz Arzallus, vol. 1 (Donostia: Gipuzkoako Foru Aldundia, 1991), 93–105.

29. It was very common to use this common saying in Basque texts of the time, see Beñat Oyharçabal, "Les prologues auctoriaux des ouvrages basques des XVIe et XVIIe siècles." *Lapurdum* 4, spec. ed. (1999): 39–94. In the same way, Esteve Materre, too, made a call for somebody else to write this doctrine in a more appropriate, beautiful type of Basque than the Basque spoken in Sara. Nor should we forget Axular's (Pedro Daguerre) advice to his readers: "this is one of the things that I would wish for, somebody to revitalize and improvise this short essay of mine, to make it better and correct the faults in it."

pretechnological mentality to be a forced conclusion.[30] On the contrary, the words he uses in the dedication seem to indicate that Etxepare's attitude reflected the point of view of a period in which printing was already very well assimilated, not a point of view of a pre-printing time or a point of view of a time when printing had been recently invented. Precisely it is due to this that he believed that the first publication in Basque was overdue: "as great men of letters have existed and exist among them [the Basques], I am amazed, my Lord, how none, for the good of his own language, has attempted to undertake or write some work in Basque so that the whole world might know that it is as good as any tongue to write in."[31]

By reading these lines, I believe it can easily be deduced that Etxepare had realized that the Basque language was being marginalized when compared to other modern languages due to the fact that it had not been printed. He praised printing in Basque because he was aware that the lack of printing would cause symbolic damage, and because he wanted to underline that printing would bring advantages to that language. He also expressed this hope, and indeed very clearly, in his stanza "Sauterelle" / "Sautrela":

> The Basques are appreciated all over the world,
> but all the rest have mocked their tongue,
> for it was not found written on any page:
> Now shall they learn what a fine thing it is.[32]

Where Did Etxepare's Literary References Come from, the French Side or the Spanish Side?

As I have observed, although they have often been compared, the works by Ruiz and Etxepare are completely different and can be said to be similar with great difficulty,[33] except for the point that—as we have seen, and

---

30. "If we leave aside his enthusiasm for printing (an enthusiasm that is typical of a pre-technological mentality), it is very easy to compare him with the Goliard poets of the fourteenth and fifteenth centuries," Juaristi, *Literatura vasca*, 37.

31. Dedication, page 115, lines 7–10.

32. "Sauterelle"/"Sautrela," page 209, lines 6–9.

33. See Gorka Aulestia, "Bernat Dechepare, escritor medieval o renacentista?"; Kortazar, "Bernard d'Etxepare bidegurutzean," and *Euskal literaturaren historia txikia*, 46; Salaberri Muñoa, *Iraupena eta lekukotasuna*, 50; and Aurélie Arcocha-Scarcia, "Les *Linguæ Vasconum Primitiæ* de Bernard Dechepare," in *Les voix de la nymphe*

as Etxaide and Mitxelena pointed out—both authors were priests, and they both used religious and amorous subject matter in their poetry.

Mitxelena's comparison presupposes that Etxepare took his literary references from Spanish literature and that his book should be classified and seen in the historical context of this literary tradition. Bearing in mind the situation of Navarre at that time, there are many reasons to accept this hypothesis. However, I am not going to pursue this line of research because if we consider *Linguæ Vasconum Primitiæ* in the context of French literature, there is no need to make such paradoxical interpretation as Mitxelena and his followers' made.

We know little about Etxepare's life, and there is not either much information about the life he spent in this part of Navarre. We can be sure that he was born and raised in Navarre—when this was still a single kingdom—where the language of administration was Spanish, which was almost certainly also the main language in Donibane Garazi (Saint-Jean-Pied-de-Port), as Gil Reicher emphasizes.[34] However, in the areas of Navarre "over the mountains" (Merindad de Ultra-Puertos), there had been strong ties with both the bishoprics of Bayonne and Dax for a long time. It is likely that, in Donibane Garazi, there was a strong influence from France and Aquitaine in cultural matters (as well as Basque influence from the two neighboring Basque areas).[35] During the first decades of the sixteenth century wars segregated the kingdom of Navarre, and Etxepare was left in the part that remained to the north of the Pyrenees Mountains. Due to the place and period in which he lived, as well as because of the position he had, he is believed to knew French, Gascon,

---

d'*Aquitaine. Ecrits, langues et pouvoirs. 1550–1610*, ed. Jean-François Courouau, Jean Cubelier, and Philippe Gardy. (Agen: Centre Mateo Bandello, 2005), 117–32.

34. Reicher states that, "civil life in Donibane Garazi looked toward Spain . . . Spanish was . . . the official language." See "Bernard Dechepare a-t-il subi des influences littéraires?" *Gure Herria* 30 (1958): 311–17.

35. Spanish influence in religious matters was felt as far away as the Bishopric of Baiona in the fifteenth century, at least in material matters. According to René Veillet, Victor Dubarat, and Jean-Baptiste Daranatz, in 1492, the Breviary of Bayonne was printed in Valencia. See René Veillet, *Recherches sur la ville et sur l'église de Bayonne: Manuscrit du Chanoine René Veillet; publié pour la première fois avec des notes et des gravures par V. Dubarat, J.-B. Daranatz* (Baiona: Lasserre; Pau: A. Lafon and Vve. Ribaut, 1910–1929), 167. It is true that there were no printing presses in the south of France at the time. See the map of late sixteenth-century presses in Western Europe in Lucien Febvre and Henri-Jean Martin, *L'apparition du livre* (Paris: Albin Michel, 1958), 266–67.

and Spanish, as well as church Latin and Basque; however, this does not tell us what his principal cultural influences were or where these cultural influences came from during the time he was writing his stanzas.

In general, those who have tried to compare Etxepare's poetry with the poetry of other authors have reached two conclusions: those who believe he was principally influenced by French cultural sources;[36] and those who believe he mainly drew on Spanish cultural influences.[37] There are also writers who observe influences from both sides (as well as from his immediate surroundings).[38]

As Aurélie Arcocha-Scarcia emphasizes,[39] the text itself only supports the first point of view because, when Etxepare mentions another language as a competitor to Basque in the "Contrapas" / "Kontrapas" stanzas, he particularly mentions French, showing that for him this was the principal language to be considered as a literary tongue.

> For no language
> Shall be found,
> be it French or any other,
> to be the equal of Basque.[40]

If Etxepare is to be situated especially in the context of Spanish literature of the time, how can it be explained that he explicitly mentions the French language in those stanzas, without even mentioning Spanish? In the same way, the fact that he had his work printed by a Bordeaux publisher seems to suggest an inclination toward French culture. This is

---

36. Michel, (1857), 48; Vinson, *Essai d'une bibliographie de la langue basque*, section 1; Gil Bera, "Melior fortuna"; Jean-Baptiste Orpustan *Précis d'histoire littéraire basque, 1545–1950. Cinq siècles de littérature en euskara* (Baigorri: Izpegi, 1996), 96; Aurélie Arcocha-Scarcia, "Bernat Etxeparekoaren maitasunezko kopletaz (1)," *Sancho el Sabio* 6 (1996); Patri Urkizu, "Bernard Lehete, Eustorg de Beaulieu eta Bernard Detxepare Errenazimenduko hiru gizon," in Jean-Claude Larronde et al., *Eugène Goyhenecheri omenaldia-hommage* (Donostia-San Sebastián: Eusko Ikaskuntza, 2001), and Salaberri Muñoa, *Iraupena eta lekukotasuna*, 50.

37. Michelena, *Historia de la literatura vasca*, 46–47; Villasante, *Historia de la literatura vasca*, section 40, 54; Sarasola, *Historia de la literatura vasca*, 38; and Juaristi, *Literatura vasca*, 33.

38. Reicher, "Bernard Dechepare a-t-il subi des influences littéraires?" and Iñaki Aldekoa, *Historia de la literatura vasca* (Donostia: Erein, 2004), 25.

39. Arcocha-Scarcia, "Les Linguæ Vasconum Primitiæ de Bernard Dechepare."

40. "Contrapas" / "Kontrapas," page 205, lines 35–38)

even more the case if what Jose Luis Orella says is true and the author was a subject of the King of Spain and, furthermore, had a Beaumont mentality,[41] and if, consequently, Etxepare was well considered in Spain. The idea that Etxepare was a medieval author totally vanishes if we take into account the parameters of French literary history. In the following section, I would like to make it clear that, while Etxepare did address some subjects that, for some authors, are representative of the medieval nature of his work, in fact these are to be situated in the early work of French Renaissance poets.[42]

Is Etxepare's Writing about Love and Women a Medieval Literary Resource?

Salaberri Muñoa considers the amorous subject matter found in some of Etxepare's stanzas to be characteristic of the Middle Ages.[43] Nevertheless, it is not easy to understand exactly what the basis for this statement is because it is unclear to what extent Etxepare's vision of amorous matters or the situations he describes in his love stanzas—which seem to have

---

41. Translator's note: To have a "Beaumont mentality" meant being pro-Spanish. Jose Luis Orella, "Mosen Bernart Dechepare," forward to Patxi Altuna's critical edition of *Lingua Vasconum Primitiæ* (Bilbao: Euskaltzaindia and Mensajero, 1980), vii–xv. I must admit that this point, in my opinion, should be looked into once more.

42. Urkizu, too, uses information provided by Bernard Lehet to demonstrate that Etxepare's protector was part of the French cultural world of the time. See "Bernard Lehete, Eustorg de Beaulieu eta Bernard Detxepare Errenazimenduko hiru gizon," in Jean-Claude Larronde et al., *Eugène Goyhenecheri omenaldia-hommage* (Donostia-San Sebastián: Eusko Ikaskuntza, 2001), 235-242.

43. Salaberri Muñoa, *Iraupena eta lekukotasuna*, 47. Juaristi accepts Kortazar's idea, in "Bernard d'Etxepare bidegurutzean," that the publication of the catechism can be considered to be a characteristic of the late Middle Ages, which raises the question of whether the presence of Christian doctrine in Etxepare's stanzas can be interpreted in the same way. I have not found any arguments to support this idea, and it is not clear in which circumstances it was developed. However, I do feel bound to say, bearing in mind the problem of contextualization here, that it is a very strange idea, not just because there was not a single publication in Basque until 1545, but also because religious teaching was not put into practice in Europe until after the invention of the printing press, particularly because of the religious problems of the sixteenth century and, for Catholics, with the approved model of teaching accepted by the Council of Trent. Although Etxepare's doctrine predated the teaching method approved by the Council of Trent (see Febvre and Martin, *L'apparition du livre*, ch. 8), it was absolutely a part of the religious upheavals that so profoundly influenced the production of books in Europe and, in my opinion, it is very difficult to see medieval characteristics in his work.

been taken as *exempla*, as Ana Maria Toledo suggests[44]—are anachronistic and, even less so, in what sense the literary resources he used reflect a link with the Middle Ages. In my opinion, if something, there is more that brings to mind the sixteenth century rather than the Middle Ages, as can be seen in many of the poems studied by Jean Haritschelhar.[45] Taking into account the type of amorous relationships between men and women described in those poems (stanzas 3–12), one might question whether the characteristics behind statements emphasizing the medieval nature of these stanzas are, in fact, to be found in the work itself. Consider, for example, the following: "While there is an erotic element in them, his [Etxepare's] love poems are not about just sexual relationships. To love is 'to serve.'"[46]

However, an examination of the text does not confirm this conclusion. If we observe all of Etxepare's stanzas that have amorous situations as their subject matter, they clearly demonstrate the aim of satisfying (men's) sexual desires, as also pointed out by Iñaki Aldekoa.[47] Taken to an extreme, this also implies using force.[48] In fact, in some of his poems, Etxepare writes that men can satisfy their needs without their wives'

---

44. Ana Maria Toledo, "Maitasun mundutarra Etxeparengan: 'Baskoen gaztiguia'," in *Euskal gramatikari eta literaturari buruzko ikerketak XXI. mendearen atarian*, vol. 2. Iker 14 (Bilbo: Euskaltzaindia, 2003). For examples of the treatment of women in French literature of the period, see Marie-Claude Malenfant, *Argumentaires de l'une et l'autre espèce de femme: le statut de l'exemplum dans les discours littéraires sur la femme (1500–1550)* (St. Nicolas, Québec: Presses de l'Université Laval, 2003).

45. Jean Haritschelhar, "*Ezkonduien koplak* (Etxepare 1545)," *Lapurdum* 7 (2002): 237–42 and "Amoros sekretuki dena," *Lapurdum* 8 (2002): 233–46.

46. Salaberri Muñoa, *Iraupena eta lekukotasuna*, 47.

47. Aldekoa, *Historia de la literatura vasca*, 27–28.

48. Or if they were forced, that would remove us even further from the spirit and the code of courtly love, and it would become an erotic game. I do not believe this interpretation is correct in Etxepare's case, but not because the subject matter would be anachronical for the time (in fact, it can easily be found in the poetry of the time). See the following poem by Clément Marot, in which the lover asks his mistress to take part in such a game: *Non que je soys ennuyé d'entreprendre / D'avoir le fruit dont le désir me poingt, / Mais je vouldrais qu'en me laissant prendre / Vous me dissiez: non, vous ne l'aurez point* (Not that I am bored of having / The fruit when I wish for it, / But I would be allowed to take it, / You saying to me, no, I do not want it). Marot, in Clément Mayer, *Clément Marot, un tableau synoptique de la vie et des œuvres de Clément Marot et des évènements artistiques, littéraires et historiques de son époque. Un choix de textes de Clément Marot* (Paris: P. Seghers, 1964), 184.

consent, for instance in "A Plea for a Kiss" / "Potaren Galdatzia." There are very few words about love in those stanzas or, to be more accurate, none at all; on the other hand, there is a very clear mention of women being upset by men's claiming their crude desires. The way women speak to the approaching men, using *toka* (a very intimate form of address when speaking with men), is an indication of the type of relationships in which they are involved: *Eia horrat, apart'adi; nor uste duk nizala?* (Go on! Begone! Who do you take me for?).[49] Finally, however, and completely beyond the courtly behavior that Aulestia mentions,[50] the man in the stanza tries violently to obtain what he wants, the woman shouting back:

That which I now desire, shall you do here.
— I truly believe you are not in jest.

Is this man going to shame me here?
— What can I do to keep you silent for a while?[51]

Many authors have argued that it would be very difficult to imagine Etxepare in the period after the Council of Trent. And that is right, because the Basque poets and prose writers from Lapurdi and Amikuze (in Lower Navarre) who taught Basque people the doctrine and the morality of the seventeenth-century Catholic Counter-Reformation offer a completely different impression. In 1545, however, that moment had not yet arrived, certainly not to that little corner of the Kingdom of Navarre. The writers of the time, including members of the church, were politically, religiously, and (probably also) culturally, under the influence of the King of France and of the court of Marguerite, Queen of Navarre. In that situation, there

---

49. Line 5, page 177. This use of *toka* is an exception in Etxepare's stanzas, in which, in all other places, women use *zuka* (a more formal form of talking with men or women). However, there is an even more significant exception in *A Hard-Hearted Lover's Scorn*. In those stanzas the woman, half way through the conversation, starts to use *toka* instead of *zuka*, to say that she has had enough of his requests.

50. "In general, these love poems are reminiscent of the courtly love themes developed by the Provençal poets," Aulestia, "Bernard Detxepare–Medieval or Renaissance Writer?" 56.

51. My interpretation of the last line differs from line 21, page 177. The interpretation of Altuna and the Morris translation supposes two things: (1) to take away the last letter in a word with *zauden* (subjunctive verb form of *egon* "stay") corrected as *zaude* (imperative), (2) that the speaking character changes in the middle of the line, something that never occurs in Etxepare's poems.

is no reason to place the figure of Etxepare outside the period he lived in, as if he were a ghost from previous centuries, because, in that cultural context, Churchmen did have the opportunity to write poetry about the sorrows and joys of love. The early French Renaissance poets lived at court, congregating around the figure of Clément Marot.[52] Mellin de Saint-Gelais (1487 or 1491–1558) was a representative of them. Being a priest and the king's chaplain, he wrote poems with what Michel Jeanneret describes as the erotic joy of the Renaissance,[53] and this term can very appropriately be used to describe Etxepare's writing in his amorous stanzas. This is what Charles Augustin Sainte-Beuve wrote a long time ago about the poetry by Mellin de Saint-Gelais:

> He does not seem to have neglected any of the contrasts that poetry could have offered with his profession and often makes use of his ecclesiastical knowledge as well as of the most profane allusions. He once wrote compliments of love on a book of hours of a penitent. (...) The portraits of Saint James, Saint Michael, Saint George, and even Saint Antony, inspired him to write more erotic quatrains than prayers, and he respected neither Mary Magdalene nor the Hundred Thousand Virgins.[54]

Let me be clear about this: by no means do I want to suggest that Etxepare found a direct source of inspiration in Saint-Gelais, because Saint-Gelais' life and work was completely different from Etxepare's. I only argue that, at the time Etxepare published his work, the poets at the French king's court, who were also known at the court of Queen Marguerite of Navarre, dared to deal with this type of subject matter (and some of them, including members of the Church, in a much cruder way than Etxepare) with no problem. There is no need whatsoever to go back to the Middle Ages to explain this phenomenon.[55]

---

52. Gérard Defaux makes it clear in his edited and annotated anthology that they make up a real group. See *Les fleurs de poésie françoyse: Hécatomphile, Société des Textes français modernes* (Paris: Société des textes français modernes, 2002).

53. Michel Jeanneret, *Eros rebelle: Littérature et dissidence à l'âge classique* (Paris: Seuil, 2003).

54. Charles Augustin Sainte-Beuve, quoted in Jules Troubat, ed., *Oeuvres de Sainte-Beuve: Tableau de la poésie française au XVIe siècle* (Paris: Garnier, 1883), 66.

55. Most of Saint-Gelais's work is compiled in *Oeuvres poétiques françaises*, ed. Donald Stone, 2 vols. (Paris: Société des textes français moderne, 1993 and 1995). After studying in Italy, he became a priest in 1524 and then a man of court. The Italian

Etxepare's attitude toward women must also be emphasized, particularly in the stanzas entitled "In Defense of Women" / "Emazten Fabore," in which his attitude corresponds to the new point of view taken by French literature, which was a continuation of the debate about the subject of women. Previously, and in line with the *Disputatio* rhetoric, authors had written sometimes in favor and sometimes against this idea. In the sixteenth century, however, the *Declamatio* had been accepted as the model, and writers used to choose one of the options:

> The Renaissance marked a turning point in the history of the dispute about women in which humanists reflected on women's status within the framework of the *Declamatio* . . . the *Declamatio* was a transposition of the judicial *Disputatio* in the realm of epideictic rhetoric, with arguments in favor and against. This transposition does not involve contradictory arguments but the adoption and the defense of a single position in the exercise of a value judgment.[56]

Etxepare also acted in that way, having chosen a particular point of view in the dispute. Furthermore, in adopting that point of view he also came to favor the prevalent attitude among French writers; in short, he was in favor of women, as is expressed in his stanzas' titles. In fact, from the sixteenth century on, the old misogynist attitudes that Etxepare did

---

influence can be seen clearly in his poems and in his surroundings. On occasion, he did have to protect himself because of having used erotic subject matter and because of having mocked the church. On this, see Henri Joseph Molinier, *Mellin de Saint-Gelays: Études sur sa vie et sur ses œuvres* (Rodez: Carrère, 1910; facs. ed., Geneva: Slatkine, 1968) and Donald Stone, *Mellin de Saint-Gelais and literary history*, French Forum Monographs 47 (Lexington, KY: French Forum, 1984). Being a friend and a member of the Marot school, he was a particular follower of the *Pléiade* group of innovative poets, and most especially of Pierre de Ronsard. Anecdotally, but also by means of emphasizing the poet's intellectual open-mindedness, it is notable that we owe to him the first specific mention in French of Copernicus's heliocentrism (though without mentioning his name and, in the following decades, being as skeptical as most other authors) three years after the publication of *On the Revolutions of the Celestial Spheres*, in his essay *Aduertissement sur les Iugemens d'astrologie, A une studieuse Damoyselle* (Notes on the Study of Astrology: A Studious Lady, 1546). On this, see Beverly S. Ridgely, "Mellin de Saint-Gelais and the First Vernacular Reference to the Copernican System in France," *Journal of the History of Ideas* 23, no. 1 (1962): 107–16.

56. Céline Marcy, "Antiféminisme et humanisme dans les Controverses des Sexes masculin et féminin de Gratien du Pont," in *L'humanisme à Toulouse (1480–1596)*, ed. Nathalie Dauvois (Paris: Champion, 2006), 378.

not like ("Do not speak ill of women, for goodness' sake,"[57]), while they did not disappear altogether, were not so prevalent in literary works. As Floyd Gray remarks, in that sense, there was a connection with some commercial reasons related to printing:

> It is certainly not incidental that the sudden popularity of pro-women literature coincides with the advent of printing, leading one to suspect that confrontation with misogynistic literature was encouraged, even exploited for commercial purposes by the printers themselves. Judging from the number of new editions of the competing works of Martin Le Franc's *Champion des Dames* and Cornelius Agrippa's *De praecellentia foeminei sexus*, La Borderie's *Amye de court*, and Antoine Heroëts's *La parfaite Amye*, it would appear that the Querelle des femmes and, more or less concurrently, the Querelle des amyes, provided ready material for one of the first successful promotional events in the history of printing in France.[58]

Although there still existed attitudes that looked down on women,[59] that period was not especially marked by such approaches in literary publications. Céline Marcy, in her study of misogynist poetry and the literature of the period on the gender dispute, emphasizes that, from the second decade of the sixteenth century on, attitudes in favor of women dominated the game of *Declamatio*: "In this case, from 1500 on, most of the works concerned with the debate of women praise them. . . . the practice of humanist *Declamatio*, often claimed in titles from the second decade of the sixteenth century, is linked to praise—praise of women then occupying an endoxical position while blaming the paradoxical position."[60]

As we have seen, there is very little reason to place Etxepare in the literary world of the Middle Ages, and even less so to consider him an example of popular culture of that time. We know very little about that

---

57. "In defense of Women" / Emazten fauore," page 157, line 1.

58. Floyd Gray, *Gender, Rhetoric and Print Culture in French Renaissance Writing* (Cambridge: Cambridge University Press, 2000), 10.

59. Malenfant, *Argumentaires de l'une et l'autre espèce de femme* (St. Nicolas, Québec: Presses de l'Université Laval), 46.

60. Céline Marcy, "Antiféminisme et humanisme dans les Controverses des Sexes masculin et féminin de Gratien du Pont," in *L'humanisme à Toulouse (1480–1596),* ed. Nathalie Dauvois (Paris: Champion, 2006), 378.

world, but it would be unlikely to find a person with little education who would write poems arguing feverously in favor of women in such a way. Whether Etxepare wrote about women or about amorous relation-ships (including stolen ones),[61] Jean-Baptiste Orpustan correctly asserts that: "Etxepare should be appreciated and considered in the spirit of his contemporaries, who were also often members of the Church and even priests or tonsured abbots, as were, for example, Rabelais and Ronsard respectively, among others."[62]

---

61. As an example of how contemporary this subject matter was, this sonnet by Mel-lin de Saint-Gelais deals with the same subject matter as "A Plea for a Kiss" / "Potaren Galdatzia" and in the same tone:

> *Non feray ; je n'en feray rien,*
> *Je ne veux point que l'on m'y touche.*
> *Laissez mon honneur; il est bien»*
> *Disoit une garce farouche*
> *A un qui dressoit l'escarmouche*
> *Tout droit sur le bord du fossé.*
> *«C'est bien rudement repoussé,*
> *Ce luy dist-il. Escoutez-moy.*
> *Qu'avez-vous? Que craignez-vous? Quoy?*
> *Que l'on vous amoindrisse et oste*
> *L'honneur de dezssoubz vostre cotte?*
> *C'est bien de quoy se tourmenter!*
> *Allez, vous n'estes qu'une sotte,*
> *Je le veux croistre et augmenter.*

> *I won't do it, I won't do a thing*
> *I do not want you to touch me there*
> *Leave me my honor, it is intact*
> *Said a timid woman of the streets*
> *To the one who arranged the meeting*
> *Directly on the bank of the moat.*
> *"That is a very harsh rejection,"*
> *He stated. "Now you listen to me.*
> *What's wrong? What are you worried about?*
> *That I will lessen and take away*
> *The honor from underneath your coat?*
> *What a silly thing to fret about!*
> *You are nothing but an idiot*
> *I want to add to and enhance that."*

(Saint-Gelais, *Oeuvres poétiques françaises*, vol. 2, 203–4). Translated by Jen Olson.

62. Orpustan, *Précis d'histoire littéraire basque, 1545–1950*, 36.

Similarly, as far as religion is concerned, nothing contradicts what I have stated here thus far. As far as I know, there has been no specific study into the contents of the stanzas that contain religious doctrine, but, according to those who have written about this, there is nothing heterodox to point out in Etxepare's doctrine. Indeed, with the impartiality of a nonbeliever, Vinson states in his bibliography that Etxepare was a good, highly orthodox Catholic.[63] However, the influences of the innovative ideas of the sixteenth-century may, perhaps, be felt at some point. It is remarkable, for example, that while the final judgment, heaven and hell, damnation, and salvation are extensively mentioned, the idea of purgatory does not appear in Etxepare's work; indeed, the very word itself is never mentioned. Of course, it is impossible to know whether this silence was deliberate or unintentional, but, bearing in mind the debates on purgatory at the time (remember that a dispute about indulgence was raging then), it may be that this silence was a consequence of such disputes.[64] The doctrine on purgatory was laid down very late, at the Councils of Lyon (1274) and Florence (1439).[65] Yet, in the south of France, to believe in it was a very widespread phenomenon from the second half of the fifteenth century on.[66] In the sixteenth century, however, the reformers did not approve of the notion of purgatory, and the Huguenots condemned and despised it. For example, in the Catechism translated by Leizarraga it is mentioned as a deceptive, groundless invention: "We know that Purgatory is an invention

---

63. Vinson, *Essai d'une bibliographie de la langue basque*, section 1a.

64. In Spain the doctrine on purgatory was very strictly controlled at the time. For example, Marcel Bataillon mentions Francisco de Enzinas's testimony that Mateo Pascual, the Archpriest of Zaragoza, had been imprisoned for a long time by the Inquisition because he had raised the question of purgatory's existence. In fact, when one of his opponents accused Pascual of this, it seems that he answered "Quid tum?" ["so what?" —trans.] And this, according to Encinas, was enough for him to be condemned (1533). See Bataillon, *Erasme et l'Espagne* (1937; new ed., forward Jean-Claude Margolin (Geneva: Droz, 1998), 515n4.

65. See Gilles Emery, "La doctrine catholique du purgatoire," *Nova et vetera* 74, no.3 (1999): 37–49.

66. See Michelle Fournié, *Le Ciel peut-il attendre? Le culte du Purgatoire dans le Midi de la France (1320 environ – 1520 environ)* (Paris: Cerf, 1997).

with no basis in Scripture, produced by the same factory of illusion and deception."[67]

Etxepare, an Uneducated Popular Poet?

It has been previously shown that the arguments in favor of the idea that Etxepare is a medieval writer are very weak and, at least in the context of French literature, one need not turn to literary anachronism in order to understand the contents of the first Basque book. In the following section, I would like to deal with another issue that is related, at least indirectly, to what has been discussed so far. Patxi Altuna presents Etxepare as a popular poet,[68] but I would like to question this idea because it does not appear to be compatible with what I previously stated.

Previous authors have shown that Etxepare's stanzas were part of a tradition, a tradition that had existed before him and was also to exist after him. In fact, this type of meter, which was based principally on assonant (8+7) meter, and which was also used after Etxepare's time,[69]

---

67. Leiçarraga, Ioannes [Joanes Leizarraga], *Iesust Christ gure Iaunaren Testamentu berria: Othoitza ecclesiasticoen forma, Fedeco confessionea* (1571; facs. ed. of Theodor Linschmann and Hugo Schuchardt's 1900 ed., Bilbao: Euskaltzaindia, 1990), 1367. Needless to say, in following doctrines (both Materre's and Etxeberri's), purgatory was put back into place. The Council of Trent confirmed the existence of purgatory. Juan Pérez de Betolaza's short bilingual *Doctrina christiana* (1596) does not mention purgatory either. However, this very short catechism is made up exclusively of lists of prayers, commandments, sins, and virtues.

68. Altuna, "Etxepare, herri poeta."

69. Both Lafon, "Sur la versification de Dechepare"; and Haritschelhar, *Le poète souletin Pierre Topet-Etchahun (1786–1862)* (Bayonne: Société des Amis du Musée Basque, 1969), 455–56, favor the 8/7 rhyme structure. On the other hand, Mitxelena, "Accentuación alta-navarra," *Fontes Linguæ Vasconum* 23 (1976): 147–62; and Altuna, *Versificación de Dechepare. Métrica y pronunciación* (Bilbao: Mensajero, 1979), 337, suggest, 4 / 4 // 4 / 3. (However, it is clear that the two suggestions do not contradict each other, with different degrees of strength being given to the pauses in the middle and a quarter way through and from the end of the lines). Vinson, "Etymologie, citations, métrique," *Revue internationale des études basques* 14, no. 2 (1923): 353–62, and Jesús María Leizaola, *Estudios sobre la poesía vasca* (Buenos Aires: Ekin, 1951), 88, see all the pauses as having the same strength: 4 / 4 / 4 / 3. Juaristi, *Literatura vasca,* 35, on the other hand, takes this poem to have sixteen syllable rhyme, a pause in the middle, and emphasis on the last syllable, which thus becomes a double: 8 / 7-1. (In any case, if the origin and comparisons are put aside, this last interpretation can be considered to support the first interpretation, as long as the last syllable's doubling is not seen to come from other languages' formal structures). Larramendi (1729, 375)

was not a mere copy of the poetry that existed at the time in the surrounding languages. In 1665, Oihenart emphasized this point when he said this about Etxepare's (8+7) meter verses: "They are all fifteen syllable verses, which can hardly be found in the works of French, Italian, and Spanish poets (whose longest verses are Alexandrines with feminine endings, which have thirteen syllables), and of which there are still fewer in Latin poetry."[70]

We can say little about the creation and the development of that tradition precisely because Etxepare is the first to offer us an example of it.[71] In that sense, then, we can take him to be a representative of Basque poetry of that time, as Oihenart himself said in 1665, specifically mentioning (as well as criticizing) Etxegarai, Logras, and Etxeberri's writing. We assume that Etxepare followed a tradition of writing Basque stanzas, a tradition that already existed although unprinted and which was almost certainly closely connected with singing. That is how, in my opinion, Etxepare's words can be interpreted—that he did not introduce Basques to the art to write stanzas, but that, rather, he took an already existing technic and used it in his own ignorant way (in other words, if we leave the writer's modesty aside, in his own manner), in order to treat of contemporary subject matter.

---

also took poetry from Lapurdi from the following century to be sixteen syllable, in particular Etxeberri's poetry.

70. Oihenart, *Art poétique basque*, 37–8. It is another matter, which does not affect the subject under discussion, whether this meter came from medieval Latin chants, as suggested by Lafon, "Sur la versification de Dechepare"; and Altuna, "Etxepare, herri poeta" and "Son hexadecasílabicos los versos de Dechepare?"; or straight from the Romance languages themselves, as argued by Mitxelena, "Accentuación alta-navarra"; and Jon Juaristi, "El Cantar de Beotibar, Un romance noticiero vasco?" *Anuario del Seminario de Filología Vasca Julio de Urquijo* 20, no. 3 (1986): 845–56 and "De métrica vascorrománica," *Anuario del Seminario de Filología Vasca Julio de Urquijo* 24, no. 2 (1990): 381–406.

71. Leizaola, *Estudios sobre la poesía vasca*, 51, states that the Song of the Battle of Beotibar was also written using the same type of meter (as I said, he defines it as 4 / 4 / 4 / 3). However, since the battle took place in the fourteenth century, it is not clear when or how this poem was set down. We only know of this poem thanks to sixteenth-century writers Esteban Garibay and Juan Martínez de Zaldibia (that is, the three stanzas which were not lost). It is also possible that the fragment that has come down to us was, in fact, from a later date. See Koldo Mitxelena, *Textos arcaicos vascos* (Madrid: Minotauro, 1964), 68; and Juaristi, "El Cantar de Beotibar, Un romance noticiero vasco?"

Altuna presents a different figure that I would like to discuss here.[72] Following Altuna's analysis, Etxepare was an uneducated popular poet who can be compared with modern bertsolaris, such as Xenpelar (nineteenth century) or Txirrita (twentieth century). Once more, this would be a paradoxical statement from the point of view of what I said previously. Altuna uses the Romantic figures of popular poets from past eras. In so doing, even though he saw this poetry's roots in the Latin Church chants of the Middle Ages,[73] in some way he excluded Basque popular poetry from literary history. This is how he could compare Etxepare with modern *bertsolaris* from three or four centuries later on. It is a remarkable fact that Altuna, by doing this comparison, accepts the idea of achronism:

> Etxepare is a popular poet, however, a popular poet in the same way that a *bertsolari* is, because he used *bertsolaritza* techniques to create his *bertsos* [verses]. He is a popular poet and a *bertsolari*, above all else, *because he is an uneducated, untrained poet*, who follows no norms laid down by masters at school, complies with no rules of verse, using hidden, deeper rules, as the *bertsolaris* do instead. Finally, *he is a* bertsolari *and not an educated poet, because he wrote his stanzas in the same way that Basques have ever done* since they started writing improvised poetry.[74]

It is true that there existed a Basque stanza tradition in the sixteenth century that used particular meters. It would appear that Altuna believes that the use of a stanza tradition in the sixteenth century with its own metric model had to be the expression of some uneducated poetic tradition, and that, aside from some particular *art poétique* like the one that would be proposed by Oihenart later, nothing else could exist. Bearing this in mind, it is possible to understood how Altuna proposed to pair up Etxepare with uneducated nineteenth-and twentieth-century bertso-

---

72. "Etxepare, herri poeta." In various authors, *Euskal linguistika eta literatura: Bide berriak* (Bilbao: Deustuko Unibertsitatea, 1981).

73. "However, what I have already said is enough to be able to place Etxepare . . . firmly within a long medieval tradition, kept up by the Church, well known in towns and in the countryside." See Altuna, "Etxepare, herri poeta," 327.

74. Altuna, "Etxepare, herri poeta," 321 (emphasis added).

laris, and to consider him in no way innovative because he was a popular poet.[75]

However, the belief that Etxepare was a humble, uneducated writer of stanzas is highly dubious because the few pieces of biographical information that we do have about him show that he was educated,[76] and his book, too, gives clear evidence of this. On the other hand, I would underline, the idea that some of his stanzas share certain characteristics with traditional songs does not inevitably lead to the conclusion that Etxepare's work was merely part of an oral tradition dating from the Middle Ages (a characteristic that is often attributed to popular poetry). I am not going to address the issue of what type of relationship there may be between Etxepare's stanzas and popular songs because people defended different points of view. Even if there were connections between the stanzas and popular songs, it cannot be inferred from this that the former were unsophisticated pieces of work. Let us be clear that in the sixteenth century (and subsequently as well) many French poems were sung, sometimes using already existing melodies, and sometimes writing new and original melodies for them, combining carefully written melodies with popular tunes.[77] Marot's case was probably the most remarkable one in this sense. Like the other poets of the time, he also often combined his poetry with songs.[78] Furthermore, they were so closely connected with traditional songs (or the songs so called, at least), that he also published a book compiling them.[79]

---

75. "Etxepare was in no way an innovator; he was, above all, a continuer and perpetuator of a popular tradition, which is the only one that survives." Ibid., 339.

76. Cf. José María Huarte, "Los primitivos del Euskera: Dechepare y su tiempo," *Euskalerriaren alde* 271 (1926): 241–48; Julio de Urquijo, "Introducción al Linguæ Vasconum Primitiæ de Bernard Dechepare (primer libro impreso en vascuence)," *Revue internationale des études basques* 24, no. 4 (1933): 660–84; and Orella, "Mosen Bernart Dechepare."

77. See Victor Graham, "Music for Poetry in France (1550–1580)," *Renaissance News* 17, no. 4 (1964): 307–17. The songs' and poems' closeness is a continuation of the Pleiade poems: on this, see especially André Verchaly, *Poésie et Air de Cour de France en France jusqu'en 1620: Musique et poésie au XVIe siècle* (Paris: Société française de Musicologie, 1953).

78. Marcel Françon, "Poésie populaire et poésie littéraire," *Modern Philology* 37, no. 1 (1939): 7–11.

79. Paul de Beaurepaire-Froment, *Bibliographie des chants populaires français*, 3rd expanded ed. (Paris: Rouart & Lerolle, 1910), 10.

At no time did Etxepare state that his stanzas were written taking into account the Basques who had received little formal education or even no education at all, contrary to the writers of Lapurdi in the following century. In his dedication, he mentioned *great men of letters* while, as we know, Axular specified the very opposite, in other words, that he was not writing for such people. And there can be no doubt, in my opinion, that when he took his work to the printers he had *educated* Basques particularly in mind, his wish being to encourage them to do just as he had done.

In this sense, I agree with Arcocha-Scarcia when she rejects that the idea that Etxepare's readers were poorly schooled.[80] Not only Altuna, Juaristi also defends such an idea. In his opinion, Etxepare wrote for farm laborers and craftsmen, who were able to hear the stanzas by means of group reading sessions.[81] However, there is not the least shred of evidence to support this hypothesis. Social subject matters very seldom appear in Etxepare's stanzas, but, when they do, they make reference to things that happened in the upper classes. This can be seen in his autobiographical poem ("The Song of Monseigneur Bernat Etxepare"), where Etxepare introduces himself as being in direct contact with the king; this is also the case, and particularly so, in The Universal Judgment / Judizio jenerala (In "The Christian Doctrine" / "Doktrina Kristiana," beginning on line 226). Even in the verses in which he makes eschatological reference to the difference between the "great" and the "small" (line 300; see also page 197, line 30), Etxepare was only mentioning groups that led society. He did not address a single word to socially humble groups, farm workers, or other simple folk. He did not have them in mind when he wrote his poetry.[82] On the contrary, he specifically defined the three groups who

---

80. Arcocha-Scarcia, "Bernat Etxeparekoaren maitasunezko kopletaz (1)."

81. "Etxepare's poems were not, then, designed to be read by individuals but to be recited and sung together in public groups made up of peasants and craftsmen (it is certainly not a book aimed at men of the Church and nobles, neither of which groups used Basque as an educated language)," Juaristi, *Literatura vasca*, 32. However, bear in mind that the same author also considers Etxepare to be an educated poet (a Church, Romance type of educated man) and not part of an oral tradition. See Juaristi, "De métrica vascorrománica."

82. Etxepare does mention poor and miserable people (page 139, lines 351–354), but only in order to underline the religious obligation of helping them.

had the power to control society:[83] armed men with political power (page 135, lines 290–292), members of the Church who controlled religious structures (page 135, lines 298–299), and, somehow between those two groups, men of letters who had power through their words (page 135, lines 294–295).[84] Those would have been the social surroundings that Etxepare had in mind when he was writing. Making use of the meters that were commonplace in the Basque Country and without merely imitating foreign models, he wanted to place his stanzas at the same level as the poetry being written in France in French, with the clear ambition to give Basque language a place of honor. And he expressed this very clearly in "Sauterelle" / "Sautrela" as well, with the rhetorical hope that *"Princes and great lords"* would wish to learn Basque:[85]

> Every Basque should raise his head,
> for his language shall be a flower
> for which Princes and great lords shall ask.
> They will desire to learn it and, if able, write it.[86]

Etxepare's *Unaffected* Language

As we accept that Etxepare made use of already known Basque stanza meter and considering his natural way of talking, is it not contradictory to place him in the context of early French Renaissance poetry? In fact, Altuna makes special use of the poet's way of talking as a basis for con-

---

83. The description that Etxepare himself gives of the Church authorities and of writers (including theologians) is particularly remarkable. I believe that this shows an element of the intellectual environment of the time, with men of letters outside the Church's direct power. It is well known that many men of letters enjoyed the patronage of the monarchs of France and Navarre at that time, and were in a sense protected by them and in their respective spheres.

84. Was that because of his post or because of legal problems? It is worth emphasizing the importance that Etxepare gave to jurists when drawing up his list of men of letters: "Jurists and theologians, poets and doctors, / attorneys, lawyers, judges and notaries (page 135, lines 294–295).

85. The significance of this objective is even clearer if we compare it with the objectives expressed by writers from Lapurdi in their texts in the following century. As far as we know, they, in contrast, knew no more than Basque because they were writing for humble people. See Oyharçabal, "Les prologues auctoriaux des ouvrages basques des XVIe et XVIIe siècles."

86. "Sauterelle" / "Sautrela," page 207, lines 10–13.

sidering him to be a popular writer: "When I state that he was a popular poet, I want to particularly emphasize that he was so not only in his use of popular verse forms, but also in his use of language."[87]

In fact, one of the arguments that links Etxepare to the popular oral tradition is based on the naturalness of his language. Altuna makes special reference to Etxepare's use of connecting words, morphology, and phonetics, and to the fact that he rarely alters the word order:

> There are no more phonetic modifications in his work than those that already existed—and that still exist today—in the spoken language: he makes use of them in the same way that they are used orally. He counts the syllables—except for small dialectical differences—basing himself on these modifications, using them freely, and carrying them out as each verse requires. He respects the phonetic groups of spoken language scrupulously and he does so by respecting the meters he uses. In fact, there are very few great forceful changes to the language or hyperbatons, and these are only used when required by the rhyme.[88]

Similarly, René Lafon, speaking in general terms, highlights Etxepare's uncluttered way of speaking, saying that his speech *was not an artificial, learned language, but the language he spoke, the local language.*[89] In other words, in his stanzas Etxepare used the people's language, fitting it to a traditional meter in a natural way. In that sense, it is no surprise that his stanzas had been compared with popular poetry.[90]

With the aim of putting Basque on the same *rank* as other languages, Etxepare used the language of his home town, Donibane Garazi, and, unlike people such as Etxeberri in the following century,[91] wrote his stan-

---

87. Altuna, *Versificación de Dechepare*, 338.

88. Ibid.

89. René Lafon, "La langue de Bernard Dechepare," *Boletín de la Real Sociedad Vascongada de Amigos del País* 7 (1951): 309–38.

90. Mitxelena states that, "in fact, the similarity of Etxepare's work with popular poetry –in spirit, language and verse form- is absolutely obvious." *Historia de la literatura vasca*, 47.

91. Even though they both used the same type of verses, there was a huge contrast between Etxepare and Etxeberri's use of rules of verse. The latter was not worried about forcing the structures of Basque to achieve aesthetic effects (in fact, Oihenart criticizes his *excessive licenses*). See Beñat Oyharçabal, "De l'usage de l'étrangeté syntaxique: les structures agrammaticales dans la versification basque du 17ème siècle." In *Erramu boneta: Festschrift for Rudolf P. G. de Rijk*, ed. Xabier Artiagoitia, Patxi Goenega,

zas without overly forcing Basque's inner structures. Mitxelena defines this language as *fluent, natural, and alive*.[92] However, why should we see the way Etxepare wrote as a sign of being an uneducated poet? It is well known that early French Rennaisance poetry used a simpler, more direct language than later poetry and, in that sense it is obvious that Etxepare also used that approach. However, and due to the fact that there are so very few contemporary Basque references, it is very difficult to gauge to what extent this is true within Basque stanza writing of the time. We should also bear in mind that, taking into account the limited social basis of written Basque at this time (and, to an extent, at least, the particularities of the language itself), the writers of Basque stanzas inevitably had to limit the way they wrote stanzas, paying special attention to the appropriateness of the assembly of their contents and ways of expressions.[93] Without using *artifice* (to use a word of the period) there was a risk of monotony and poetic poverty, which could only be overcome by the poet's skill (Joachim du Bellay defines this as *allégresse d'esprit* or a happy spirit in note 94 below). To some extent, this happened with Etxepare, at least for some observers.[94]

The idea that Etxepare was an uneducated poet has deep roots in the modest history of Basque literary criticism. Indeed, in chapter 14 of the second edition of *Notitia utriusque Vasconiæ* (1656), Oihenart criticizes "vulgar versifiers" as being writers that are unable to differentiate between male and female rhymes, and mentions the first rhymes of "Lovers' Quarrel" / "Amorosen Disputa" (although without mentioning

---

and Joseba A. Lakarra. Anejos del Anuario del Seminario de Filología Vasca "Julio de Urquijo" 44 (Leioa: Universidad del País Vasco, Servicio Editorial-Euskal Unibertsitatea, Argitalpen Zerbitzua, 2002).

92. Mitxelena, *Historia de la literatura vasca*, 46.

93. It must be emphasized that the few attempts made with a different approach, specially by using *tekné*, also failed in the following periods. Thus, following Etxeberri, very few writers went beyond syntax or broke it up in order to write their stanzas. Nor was Oihenart very successful in trying to define a Basque meter (types of meter) in a strict, limiting way, wanting to restrict the options given by the language's morphological and phonological rules. In the same way, the imitative model proposed by Larramendi in the following century, distancing itself from the usual ways of speech, had very few followers. See the sonnet (1729, p. 391) and the ten-line poem (idem., p. 393) at the end of *El impossible vencido*.

94. Reicher, "Bernard Dechepare a-t-il subi des influences littéraires?"; Mitxelena, "Sarrera gisa"; Sarasola, *Historia de la literatura vasca*; and Altuna, *Versificación de Dechepare*.

the author's name) as an example of such a failure. The same criticism was repeated in the *Art poétique basque* (1665). However, Oihenart had very marked and restricted ideas about how well-written Basque poetry should be like, and what he said in no way really demonstrates that Etxepare's stanzas were unskilled; it only demonstrates that, besides the fact that they belonged to different centuries, the two poets had different points of view about how stanzas should be written and how poetry should comply with formal stipulations.

Looking at French poetry of the time once more, one can see that the members of the group of poets known as the *Pléiade*, and specially du Bellay (1549), is critical of more or less the same things, and that they especially rejected poets who did not use or who looked down on *artifice* and *doctrine*.[95] As French and Basque poetry were so different in scale and in their histories at that time, it would make no sense to take this comparison seriously, but I believe that it somehow helps in placing Etxepare in his context. Similarly, one could easily apply to Etxepare what Joachim du Bellay wrote of Marot: "He is easy (to read) and seldom strays from the usual way of speaking."[96]

Thus, was Etxepare a popular poet or not? It depends on what is meant by popular poetry. If one takes Altuna's notion of the idea and its connotations (according to which popular poets are uneducated poets, simple people who write unpolished stanzas in the way they have always been written), it is hard to suggest that Etxepare's stanzas could be defined in that way. Etxepare was an educated man who wished to give Basque an honorable place in the literary world, and who tried to do

---

95. "Let no one argue the case of some among us, who have had much of an echo in our vulgar language, although they have no doctrine or at least none other than a mediocre one. Let no one argue the point, likewise, that poets are born, because that implies the ardor and happy spirit that naturally excite the poets, and without which any doctrine would for them be hollow and useless. It would, to be sure, be too easy and yet contemptible on account of it being an eternal flame if the bliss of nature given to even the ignoramus was enough to make something worthy of immortality. . . . Whoever wishes to live in the memory of posterity must sweat and tremble time and time again, and so far as our court poets drink, eat, and sleep at ease, endure hunger, thirst, and long vigils." Joachim du Bellay, *Deffence et illustration de la langue françoise* (Paris: Arnoul l'Angelier, 1549), vol. 2, chap. 3. Available on the Gallica website at http://gallica.bnf. fr/ark:/12148/bpt6k1050733

96. Joachim du Bellay, *Deffence et illustration de la langue françoise* (Paris: Arnoul l'Angelier, 1549), bk. 2, ch. 1. Available on the *Gallica* website at http://gallica.bnf.fr/ark:/12148/bpt6k1050733.

so by writing and printing his stanzas and using various contemporary subject matters when producing them. By publishing poetry in Basque, and so bringing the language into the same arena as other languages, he was exceptionally aware that he was opening up a new path for Basques in the world of writing.[97] It is also due to this, particularly if we take into consideration the first part of the century, that Etxepare may undoubtedly be considered a poet of his age and, as Jean Haritschelhar states, he was completely a man of the sixteenth century.

Bibliography

Aldekoa, Iñaki. *Historia de la literatura vasca*. Donostia: Erein, 2004.

Altamira, Rafael. *Historia de España y de la civilización española*. 4th edition, reprint. Foreword by J. M. Jover. 2 volumes. Barcelona: Crítica, 2001.

Altuna, Francisco [Patxi]. *Versificación de Dechepare. Métrica y pronunciación*. Bilbao: Mensajero, 1979.

———. "Etxepare, herri poeta." In Various Authors, *Euskal linguistika eta literatura: Bide berriak*. Bilbao: Deustuko Unibertsitatea, 1981.

———. "Son hexadecasílabicos los versos de Dechepare?" In *Memoriæ Mitxelena Magistri Sacrum*, edited by Joseba Lakarra and Iñigo Ruiz Arzallus. Volume 1. Donostia: Gipuzkoako Foru Aldundia, 1991.

Arcocha-Scarcia, Aurélie. "Bernat Etxeparekoaren maitasunezko kopletaz (1)." *Sancho el Sabio* 6 (1996): 211–34.

———. "Les *Linguæ Vasconum Primitiæ* de Bernard Dechepare." In *Les voix de la nymphe d'Aquitaine. Ecrits, langues et pouvoirs. 1550–1610*, edited by Jean-François Courouau, Jean Cubelier, and Philippe Gardy. Agen: Centre Mateo Bandello, 2005.

Ariztimuño, José. "El primer renacentista y poeta euskeldun." *Yakintza* 1 (1933): 12–20.

Aulestia, Gorka. "Bernat Dechepare—Medieval or Renaissance Writer?" In *The Basque Poetic Tradition*. Translation by Linda White. Reno: University of Nevada Press, 2000.

---

97. See Arcocha-Scarcia, "Bernat Etxeparekoaren maitasunezko kopletaz (1)," 221, who makes this point clearly when analyzing the adverbs of time in "Contrapas."

Bataillon, Marcel. *Erasme et l'Espagne*. 1937; new edition with a forward by Jean-Claude Margolin. Geneva: Droz, 1998.

Beaurepaire-Froment, Paul de. *Bibliographie des chants populaires français*, 3rd expanded edition. Paris: Rouart & Lerolle, 1910.

Bellay, Joachim du. *Deffence et illustration de la langue françoise*. Paris: Arnoul l'Angelier, 1549. Available on the *Gallica* website at http://gallica.bnf.fr/ark:/12148/bpt6k1050733.

Defaux, Gérard. *Les fleurs de poésie françoyse. Hécatomphile, Société des Textes français modernes*, Paris: Société des textes français modernes, 2002.

Díaz-Plaja, Guillermo, ed. *Historia general de las literaturas hispánicas*. Volume 5. Barcelona: Barna, 1958.

Echepare, Bernard. *Linguæ Vasconum Primitiæ*. Critical edition edited by Patxi Altuna. 1545; reprint, Bilbo: Euskaltzaindia and Mensajero, 1980.

Etxaide, Yon. *Amasei seme Euskalerriko*. Kuliska sorta 21–22. Zarautz: Itxaropena, 1958.

Emery, Gilles. "La doctrine catholique du purgatoire." *Nova et vetera* 74, no.3 (1999): 37–49.

Febvre, Lucien, and Henri-Jean Martin. *L'apparition du livre*. Paris: Albin Michel, 1958.

Fournié, Michelle. *Le Ciel peut-il attendre? Le culte du Purgatoire dans le Midi de la France (1320 environ – 1520 environ)*. Paris: Cerf, 1997.

Françon, Marcel. "Poésie populaire et poésie littéraire." *Modern Philology* 37, no. 1 (1939): 7–11.

———. "Ronsard et la poésie populaire." *Modern Language Notes*, 65, no. 1 (1950): 55–57.

Gil Bera, Eduardo. "Melior fortuna." *Mazantini* 2 (1992). Available on the Armiarma website at http://andima.armiarma.com/maza/maza0208.htm.

Graham, Victor. "Music for Poetry in France (1550–1580)." *Renaissance News* 17, no. 4 (1964): 307–17.

Gray, Floyd. *Gender, Rhetoric and Print Culture in French Renaissance Writing*. Cambridge: Cambridge University Press, 2000.

Haritschelhar, Jean. *Le poète souletin Pierre Topet-Etchahun (1786–1862)*, Bayonne: Société des Amis du Musée Basque, 1969.

———. "Emazten fabore." In *Euskal gramatikari eta literaturari buruzko ikerketak XXI. mendearen atarian*. Volume 2. Iker 14. Bilbo: Euskaltzaindia, 2003.

———. "Défense et illustration de la langue basque au XVIe siècle: La *Sautrela* de Bernat Echapare." *Hommage à Jacques Allières, I. Domaine basque et pyrénéen*, edited by Michel Aurnague and Michel Roché Anglet. Biarritz: Atlantica, 2002.

———. "*Ezkonduien koplak* (Etxepare 1545)." *Lapurdum* 7 (2002): 237–42.

———. "*Amoros sekretuki dena*." *Lapurdum* 8 (2002): 233–46.

Huarte, José María. "Los primitivos del Euskera. Dechepare y su tiempo." *Euskalerriaren alde* 271 (1926): 241–48.

Jeanneret, Michel. *Eros rebelle. Littérature et dissidence à l'âge classique.* Paris: Seuil, 2003.

Juaristi, Jon. "El Cantar de Beotibar, Un romance noticiero vasco?" *Anuario del Seminario de Filología Vasca Julio de Urquijo* 20, no. 3 (1986): 845–56.

———. *Literatura vasca.* Madrid: Taurus, 1987. New edition, Donostia: Erein 2001.

———. "De métrica vascorrománica." *Anuario del Seminario de Filología Vasca Julio de Urquijo* 24, no. 2 (1990): 381–406.

Kortazar, Jon. "Bernard d'Etxepare bidegurutzean." *Entseiukarrean* 12 (1996): 29–35.

———. *Euskal literaturaren historia txikia. Ahozkoa eta klasikoa (XVI–XIX).* 2nd edition. Donostia: Erein, 2000.

Lafitte, Pierre. *Eskualdunen loretegia.* Baiona: Lasserre, 1931.

———. *La littérature basque en Labourd, Basse-Navarre et Soule.* Bayonne: Librairie Le Livre, 1941.

Lafon, René. "La langue de Bernard Dechepare." *Boletín de la Real Sociedad Vascongada de Amigos del País* 7 (1951): 309–38.

———."Notes pour une édition critique et une traduction française des *Linguæ Vasconum Primitiæ* de Bernard Dechepare." *Boletín de la Real Sociedad Vascongada de Amigos del País* 8 (1952): 139–80.

———. "Sur la versification de Dechepare." *Boletín de la Real Sociedad Vascongada de Amigos del País* 13 (1957): 387–93.

Larramendi, Manuel. *El impossible vencido. Arte de la lengua bascongada.* Salamanca: Antonio Joseph Villargordo Alcaráz, 1729.

Leizaola, Jesús María. *Estudios sobre la poesía vasca.* Buenos Aires: Ekin, 1951.

Leiçarraga, Ioannes [Joannes Leizarraga]. 1571. *Iesust Christ gure launaren Testamentu berria.* Facsimile of Theodor Linschmann and Hugo Schuchardt's 1900 edition. Bilbo: Euskaltzaindia, 1990.

Malenfant, Marie-Claude. *Argumentaires de l'une et l'autre espèce de femme: le statut de l'exemplum dans les discours littéraires sur la femme (1500–1550).* St. Nicolas, Québec: Presses de l'Université Laval, 2003.

Marcy, Céline. "Antiféminisme et humanisme dans les *Controverses des Sexes masculin et féminin* de Gratien du Pont." In *L'humanisme à Toulouse (1480–1596),* edited by Nathalie Duvois. Paris: Champion, 2006.

Mayer, Clément. *Clément Marot, un tableau synoptique de la vie et des œuvres de Clément Marot et des évènements artistiques, littéraires et historiques de son époque. Un choix de textes de Clément Marot.* Paris: P. Seghers, 1964.

Marot, Clément. *Les oeuvres de Clément Marot de Cahors, valet de chambre du roy... augmentées de deux livres d'Épigrammes, et d'ung grand nombre d'aultres oeuvres par cy devant non imprimées, le tout soigneusement par luy mesmes reveu et mieulx ordonné,* Lyon: M. Dolet, 1538. Available on the French National Library's website: http://gallica.bnf.fr/ark:/12148/bpt6k70238n.

Michel, Francisque. *Le Pays Basque. Sa population, sa langue, ses moeurs, sa littérature et sa musique.* Paris: F. Didot, 1857.

Michelena, Luis [Koldo Mitxelena]. *Historia de la literatura vasca.* Madrid: Minotauro, 1960.

———. *Textos arcaicos vascos.* Madrid: Minotauro, 1964.

———. "Sarrera gisa." In Bernard Dechepare, *Olerkiak: 1545.* San Sebastián: Edili, 1968.

———. "Accentuación alta-navarra." *Fontes Linguæ Vasconum* 23 (1976): 147–62.

Molinier, Henri Joseph. *Mellin de Saint-Gelays: études sur sa vie et sur ses œuvres* Rodez: Carrère, 1910; facsimile edition, Geneva: Slatkine, 1968.

Oihenart, Arnaud. *Art poétique basque.* 1665; reprint, manuscript published by Pierre Lafitte in *Gure Herria,* supplement (1967).

Orella, Jose Luis. "*Mosen Bernart Dechepare.*" Forward to Patxi Altuna's critical edition of *Lingua Vasconum Primitiæ.* Bilbao: Euskaltzaindia & Mensajero, Bilbao, 1980.

Orixe [Nikolas Ormaetxea]. *Euskal literaturaren historia laburra.* 1927; reprint, edited by Paulo Iztueta. Donostia: Utriusque Vasconiæ, 2002.

Orpustan, Jean-Baptiste. "Bernat Etxepare 'ta Arnalde Oihenart: ondoriotasunetarik harat." *Iker* 8 (1993): 451–66.

———. *Précis d'histoire littéraire basque, 1545–1950. Cinq siècles de littérature en euskara.* Baigorri: Izpegi, 1996.

Oyharçabal, Beñat. "Les prologues auctoriaux des ouvrages basques des XVIe et XVIIe siècles." *Lapurdum* 4, special edition (1999): 39–94.

———. "De l'usage de l'étrangeté syntaxique: les structures agrammaticales dans la versification basque du 17ème siècle." In *Erramu boneta: Festschrift for Rudolf P. G. de Rijk,* edited by Xabier Artiagoitia, Patxi Goenega, and Joseba A. Lakarra. Anejos del Anuario del Seminario de Filología Vasca "Julio de Urquijo" 44. Leioa: Universidad del País Vasco, Servicio Editorial-Euskal Unibertsitatea, Argitalpen Zerbitzua, 2002.

Reicher, Gil. "Bernard Dechepare a-t-il subi des influences littéraires?" *Gure Herria* 30 (1958): 311–17.

Ridgely, Beverly S. "Mellin de Saint-Gelais and the First Vernacular Reference to the Copernican System in France." *Journal of the History of Ideas* 23, no. 1 (1962): 107–16.

Ruiz, Juan. *El Libro de Buen Amor.* Alicante: Biblioteca Virtual Miguel de Cervantes, 2000. Available online at http://www.cervantesvirtual.com/FichaObra.html?Ref=2765.

Saint-Gelais, Mellin de. *Oeuvres complètes de Melin de Saint-Gelais.* Edited by Prosper de Blanchemain. Volume 2. Paris: 1873; reprint, Nendeln, Lichtenstein: Kraus, 1970. Both volumescan be read on the *Gallica* website.

———. *Oeuvres poétiques françaises.* Edited by Donald Stone. 2 Volumes. Paris: Société des textes français moderne, 1993 and 1995.

Salaberri Muñoa, Patxi. *Iraupena eta lekukotasuna. Euskal literatura idatzia 1900 arte.* Donostia: Elkar, 2002.

Sarasola, Ibon. "Euskal poesia gaur." *Jakin* 24 (1967): 12–19.

————. *Historia de la literatura vasca.* Madrid: Akal, 1976.

Stone, Donald. *Mellin de Saint-Gelais and literary history.* French Forum Monographs 47. Lexington, KY: French Forum, 1984.

Toledo, Ana Maria. "Maitasun mundutarra Etxeparengan: 'Baskoen gaztiguia'." *Euskal gramatikari eta literaturari buruzko ikerketak XXI. mendearen atarian.* Volume 2. *Iker* 14. Bilbo: Euskaltzaindia, 2003.

Troubat, Jules, ed. *Oeuvres de Sainte-Beuve. Tableau de la poésie française au XVIe siècle.* Volume 1. Paris: Garnier, 1883.

Urkizu, Patri, ed. *Historia de la literatura vasca.* Madrid: UNED ediciones, 2000.

————. "Bernard Lehete, Eustorg de Beaulieu eta Bernard Detxepare Errenazimenduko hiru gizon." In Jean-Claude Larronde et al., *Eugène Goyhenecheri omenaldia-hommage.* Donostia: Eusko Ikaskuntza, 2001.

Urquijo, Julio de. "Introducción al *Linguæ Vasconum Primitiæ* de Bernard Dechepare (primer libro impreso en vascuence)." *Revue internationale des études basques* 24, no. 4 (1933): 660–84.

Veillet, René. *Recherches sur la ville et sur l'église de Bayonne. Manuscrit du Chanoine René Veillet; publié pour la première fois avec des notes et des gravures par V. Dubarat, J.-B. Daranatz.* Bayonne: Lasserre; Pau: A. Lafon and Vve. Ribaut, 1910–1929.

Verchaly, André. *Poésie et Air de Cour de France en France jusqu'en 1620. Musique et poésie au XVIe siècle.* Paris: Société française de Musicologie, 1953.

Villasante, Luis. *Historia de la literatura vasca.* 1961; reprint, Oñati: Arantzazu, 1979.

Vinson, Julien. *Essai d'une bibliographie de la langue basque,* Paris: Maisonneuve, 1891; reprint, with a forward by Luis Michelena, with the volume added in 1898 and corrected, *Bibliographie de la langue basque.* 2 volumes. San Sebastián: Seminario de Filología Vasca "Julio de Urquijo" de la Excelentísima Diputación Foral de Guipúzcoa, 1984.

————. "Etymologie, citations, métrique." *Revue internationale des études basques* 14, no. 2 (1923): 353–62.

Linguæ Vasconum Primitiæ

The First Fruits of the Basque Language, 1945

Facsimile

LINGVAE VASCONVM PRIMI-
tiæ per Dominum Bernardum Dechepare
Rectorem sancti michælis veteris.

¶Aduertant Impreſſor, & lectores quod.z.nunquam
ponitur pro.m. Neꝗ.t. ante.i. pronunciatur pro.c. Et
vbi virgula ponitur ſub.ç.hoc modo quod ſit dum præ
ponitur vocalibus.a.o.u.Tunc.c.pronunciabitur paulo
aſperius quam.z.vt in.ce.ci.

Rregueren aduocatu videzco eta noblea
ri virthute eta honguciez complituy ari
bere iaun eta iabe Bernard Leheteri ber
nard echeparecoac haren cerbitzari chi
piac gogo honez goraynci baque eta of-
fagarri Ceren bafcoac baitira abil animos eta gentil
eta hetan içan baita eta baita fciencia gucietan lettratu
hahdiric miraz nago iauna nola batere ezten affayatu
bere lengoage propriaren fauoretan heufcaraz cerbait
obra eguitera eta fcributan imeitera ceren ladin publi
ca mundu gucietara berce lengoagiac beçala hayn fcri
batzeco hondela. Eta caufa honegatic gueldit zenda a-
bataturic eceyn reputacione vague eta berce nacione
oroc vfte dute ecin denfere fcriba dayteyela lengoage
hartan nola berce oroc baitu te fcribatzen beryan Eta
ceren oray çuc iauna noble et naturazcoac beçala bay
tuçu eftimatzen goratzen eta ohoratzen heufcara çuri neure iaun eta iabia beçala igorten darauritzut heu
fcarazco copblabatzu ene ignoranciaren araura eguinac. Ceren iauna hayec iqhuffiric eta corregituric pla
zer duçun beçala irudi baçautzu imprimi eraci diçaçun eta çure efcutic oroc dugum ioya ederra Imprimituric heufcara orano içan eztena eta çure hatfe honetic dadin aitzinerat augmenta continua eta publica
mundu gucietara eta bafcœc bercec beçala duten bere lengoagian fcribuz cerbait doctrina eta plazer harceco folaz eguiteco cantatzeco eta denbora igaraiteco
materia eta ginendirenec gueio duten caufa oboro ha
ren abançatzeco eta obligatu guiren guciac geyncoari
A ij

othoyz eguitera dizum mundu honeten profperoqui
vicia eta bercian parabiçuy a,   Amen.

¶ Doctrina Christiana.

unduy áden guiçon oroc beharluque péfatu
Iangoycoac nola duyen batbedera formatu
Bere irudi propiara gure arima creatu
Memoriaz vorondatez endelguy az goarnitu.

Eceyn iaunec eztu nahi muthilgaixtoa eduqui
Ez pagatu foldataric cerbiçatu gaberic
Iangoycua ariduçu hala hala gurequi
Gloriar ic ez emanen hongui eguin gaberic

Muthilec gure cerbiçut an deramate vrthia
Soldata apphur bategatic harcen pena handia
Iangoycoac beharluque guc veçanbat valia
Cerbiçatu behardugu emaytecoz gloria.

Oguiric eztacuffat vilcen haci ereyn gaberic
Norc cerbaci ereyn vilcendici çomunqui
Obra honac vqhenendu goalardona frangoqui
Bay etare beqhatuyac punicione fegurqui.

Ceren ieyncoa egun oroz ongui ari bayçaygu
Gucere hala behardugu harçaz vnfa orhitu
Gure h atfeeta fina hura dela penfatu
Goyz etarrax orhituqui haren icena laudatu.
Arraxian
Arraxian ecitian gomendadi ieyncoary
Eta othoy beguireçan perilgucietaric

Guero iraçar adinian orhit adi vertaric
Cenbaitere oracione erraytera deuotqui
        Goycian
Albadaguic ioanadi eliçara goycian
Ieyncoari han gomenda bere eche faynduyan
Han farcian penfa eçac aycinian norduyan
Norequila minço yçan han agoen artian.
        Ilherrian
Hilez vnfa orhit adi ilherrian farçian
Hi nolaco ciradela viciciren artian
Hec veç ala hil beharduc eta ez iaquin orduya
Othoy eguic ieyncoari deyen varcamenduya.
        Batheyarria
Eliçara içanian foeguic bateyarrira
Penfa eçac handuyala recebitu fedia
Ieyncoaren gracia eta faluaçeco vidia
Hari eguin albaiteça lehen eçagucia.
        Gorpuz faynduya
Vertan guero fo albaitegui nōden gorpuz fainduya
Penfa eçac hura dela hire faluaçaha
Adoreçac deuocionez eta galde gracia
Azquen finian emandiaçan recebice dignia.
        Curucea
Crucifica iqhus eta orhit adi orduyan
Nola yçan redemitu haren odol faynduyaz
Harc eryo haritudic hiri leyan vicia
Penfa ezac nola eman hari vere ordia.
        Andredona Maria
Andere honaden leqhura ailchaiçac veguiac

Mundu oro eztaquidic hura veçayn valia
Ieyncoaren hurranena hura diagoc glorian
Graciac oro vere efcuyan nahiduyen orduyan.

Oandere gloriofa eta ama eztia
çutan dago beqhatoren fperança gucia
Ni çugana nyatorqueçu beqhatore handia
Arimaren faluacera çu çaquiztan valia.
Saynduyer
Saynduyer ere eguin eçac heure eçagucia
Singularqui nortan vaytuc heure deuocionia
Ceyn faynduren ve fta daten orhit egun verian
Eta noren ycenetanfundatuden eliça
Orhituquiothoy eguindaquizquian valia
Oracione igandeco
Mifericordiaz bethe ciraden iaun eztia
Othoy ençun yaçadaçu neure oracionia
Biciniçan artian eta erioco phunduyan
çuc ydaçu othoy offo neure endelgamenduya
Alteratu gabetaric çure fede faynduyan
Gaucen vnfa eguiteco neure azquen finian.

Eta orduyan çuc ydaçu indar eta gratia
Beccatuyez vqheyteco vide dudan doluya
Perfectuqui eguiteco neure confeffionia
Neure beqhatuyez oroz dudan varqhamenduya
Bay dignequi errecebi çure gorpuz faynduya
Bayetare vehardiren verce fagramenduyac.
Exay gayça ginen vayta tentaceraorduya

Nontic engana niroyen vere arte guciaz
Othoy iauna enguztaçu lagun çure faynduyae
Enexayac venci enaçan neure azquen finian.

Ene arima orJuyan har othoy çure glorian
Nola vaita redemitu çure odol fayndu yaz
Eta nic handacuffadan çure veguitartia
Eta fayndu yequilauda çure mageftatia

Goyz etarrafti eguitenduc buluz etavezticia
Gorpuçaren cerbiçutan barazcari afaria
Arimaren faluaçeco ieyncoaren ohorian
Eçayala othoy neque gauça hoyen eguitia
Egunoroz ecin vada afteoroz igandian

Gure artian haur dacusfat ixutarçum handia
Nola dugun cerbiçacen hanbat gure exaya
Iangoycua defconoci gure faluaçalia
Eta oroc eçagucen dela videgabia

Anhiz gendez miraz nago neureburuyaz lehenic
Nola gauden mūdu hunequi hayn vorthizqui iofficic
Hanbat gende dacufcula hunec enganaturic
Oranocoac ygorritu oro buluzcorriric
Eta eztute guerocoec hantic efcapaceric

Perfonoro hildenian hirur çathi eguiten
Gorpuzori vftelcera lur hoçian egoyzten
Vnharçuna ahaidiec vertan dute particen

Arima gaixoa dabilela norat ahaldaguien
Hayrrviage vortician compaynia faltacen

Orhituqui ygandian vehardugu penfatu
Cenbatetan eguin dugun afte hartan beccatu
Orhit eta ieyncoari barqhamendu efcatu
Atorra nola arimere afte oroz garbitu.

Bi pundutan diagoçu gure gauça gucia
Hongui eguin vadaçagu fegur parabiçuya
Beqhatutan hildadina bertan comdenatuya
Berce videric ecin date hobenari beguira.

Ehonere eztacufat hayn laxoden arçaynic
Oxoa hencen eztuyenic bere ardietaric
Gure arimaz cargu dugu iangoycuac emanic
Nola gobernacendugun batbederac fobegui
Condu herfi vehardugu harçaz eman fegurqui
Nori baitu vereodolaz carioqui eroffi
Hala cinex eztaçana dauque enganaturic.

Contemplatu vehardugu paffione faynduya
Eta fendi vihocian haren pena handia
Nola çagoen curucian oro çauriz bethia
Huyn efcuyac içaturic eta vuluzcorria

Ohoynequi vrcaturic nola gayzquiguilia
Eta arhancez coroaturic mundu ororen iabia
Haren gorpuz preciofo eta delicatuya

B

Gayzqui efcarniaturic eta çathicatuya.

Elas orduyan nola çagoen haren arima triſtia
Haren ama maytia eta mundu ororen habia
Pena hetan ecuſteaz bere feme maytia
Eta hilcen veguietan mundu ororen vicia.

Viocian dirauſtaçu guertuz ama eztia
çure orduco doloriac eta vihoz çauriac
Beguiez nola cenacufan çure iabe handia
Orotaric laryola odol preciatuya
Hec nigatic ciradela arinuçu qhonduya.

Orhit adi nola duyan eguin anhiz beqhatu
Heyen caufaz merexitu anhicetan hondatu
Bere mifericordiaz nola huyen guardatu
Eta dolu vqhen vaduc vertan oro barqhatu
Eta aguian hic eguinen vertan verriz beqhatu.

Orhit adi iengoycoaren mageſtate handiaz
Ceruya lurra ychafoa daduçala efcuyan
Saluacia damnacia eryoa eta vicia
Eſtendicen orotara haren poteſtatia
Eci efcapa hari ehor dauguinian manuya.

Mundu honetan vadirogu batac bercia engana
Bana vercian eguiatic bat bedera ioanenda
Nor nolaco içan guiren orduyan aguerico da
Eguin erran penfatuyac aguerico guciac.

Orhit adi ieyncoaren iufticia handiaz
Nola oroc vehardugun eman qhondu herfia
Eguin oroz recebitu gure merexitu ya
Eryoa dauguinian vayta haren meçu ya.

Ordu hartan afer date hari apellacia
Harc ehori eztemayo oren vaten epphia
Ecet are eftimacen chipia ez handia
Bat vederac egarrico orduyan vere haxia.

Orduyan cer eguinendut gaixo beqhataria
A rartecoac faltaturen contra iuge handia
Abocacen eztaquique ehorc haren gortian
Oguen oro publicoqui aguerturen orduyan.

Elas othoy oroc eguin oray penitencia
Behar orduyan eztuquegu guero aguian aizina
Anhiz iende enganatu doa luçamendu yaz
Seguraturic ehorc eztu egun vaten vicia.

Guguirade egun oroz heryoaren azpian
Behardugu preft eduqui gure gauça gucia
Gure gaucez ordenatu offo guiren artian
Guero eztugun eguiteco heçaz azquen finian
Arimaz afqui eguiteco vaduquegu orduyan.

Penfa othoy nola gauden bi bideren erdian
Salua bano damnaçeco perileco pundu yan
Ehor fida eztadila othoy vanitatian

Saynduy ac eçiraden farthu vanitatez glorian.

Elas othoy hunat veha beqhatore gucia
Beqhatu yaz damnacendu iangoycuac munduya
Ceren hanbat veccatutan deramagu vicia
Eta guhaurc gure faltaz galcen gureburuya.

Arzayn oroc vilcenditu ardiac arraxaldian
Leqhu honerat eramayten eguraldi gáycian
Bat bederac penfa veça arimaren gaynian
Nola faluaturen duen hura vere finian.

Beqhatorec yfernuyan dute pena handia
Pena handi ycigarri eceyn paufu gabia
Seculacoz egon vehar hango fugar vician
çuhur denac hara eztohen eguin penitencia.
　　　　Harmac eryoaren contra
Eryoa iauguitenda guti vfte denian
Eta aguian ez emanen confeffione epphia
Hirur gauça albaditu ehorc ere eguiaz
Nola ere hil vaytadi doha faluamenduyan.
　　　　Lehen eguia
O iaun hona aytor cendut beqhatore niçala
Eta gaizqui eguitiaz oguen handi dudala
Nic vaycitut offenfatu bide eztudan veçala
Dolu dicit eta damu çure contra eguinaz.
　　　　Bigarren eguia
Oiaun hona gogo dicit oren prefent honetan
Goardaceco beqhaturic vici niçan artian

Othoy iauna çuc ydaçu indar eta gracia
Gogo honetan yrauteco neure vici gucian.
Heren eguia
Oiaun hona gogo dicit gariçuma denian
Eguiazqui eguiteco neure confeſſionia
Vav etare compliceco didan penitencia
Othoy iauna çuc confirma ene vorondatia.

Eta hoyec eguiazqui ehorc hala ezpaditu
Albayliaqui duda gabe ecin dateyela ſalbu
Bere beqhatu yac oro vaditu ere confeſſatu
Eta hala çinhex beça nahi eztenac enganatu.

Apezeq ez apezpicuq ez etare aytaſaynduc
Abſoluacen halacoaren eceyn bothereric eztu
Iangoycua bethiere vihocera ſodiagoçu
Guhaurc vano ſegurago gure gogua diacuxu
Gogua gabe hura vaytan hiçac oro afertuçu.

Regla eçac egun oroz onſa heure etchia
Eure gauça gucietan emac diligencia
Eta eure trabayluyaduyan penitencia
Iangoycua lauda eçac gauça ororen buruyan.

Honequila albay teça bethiere conuerſa
Gaixtœqui ecin ayte gayzqui beci prouecha
Bercer eguin eztaçala nahi eçuqueyena
Ez etare ſalta ere hiaurc nahi duyana
Legue honi ſegui vedi ſalbu nahiduyena.

¶Hamar manamenduyac:
Doreçac iągoycobat onheſtz oroz gaynetiç
Haren ycena ez iura cauſa gabe vanoqui
Ygandiac eta veſtac ſanĉtifica deuotqui
Ayta eta ama ohoraiçac vici yçan lucequi
Ehor erho eztaçala ez etare gaycetſi
Norc veria vayecila emazteric ez hunqui
Vercerena eztaçala ebaxi ez eduqni
Fama gayciq eztemala lagunari falſuqui
Bercen emazte alabac ez deſira gayxtoqui
Eçetare vnhaſuna lecotbedi iuſtoqui.

Manamenduyac hoyec dira iangoycuac emanic
Hoc veguira diç agula ſalua guiten hegatic.
    ¶Iudicio generala
Iudicio generalaz nola orhit eztira
Beccatutan vici dira bethi vere ayſira
Egun hartan gal ezquiten aycinetic veguira
Han orduyan eztuquegn ehorc ere ayzina
Harçan vnſa orhitcia çuhurcia handida.

Arma arma mundu oro iudicio handira
Ceru eta lur ororen creadore handia
Munduyaren iuyacera rigoroſqui helduda
Nola gauden apphaynduric bat bederac beguira.

Manamendu ygortendu mundugucietaric
Gende oro bat daquion ioſafaten vilduric
Ehonere ehorere eſcapatu gaberic.

Ceru eta lur gucia daude yqharaturic.

Eryoa manacendu eceyn falta gaberic
Hilac oro dacacela aycinera viciric
Hantic harat eztuquela vothereric iagoytic
Mundu oro iarrirenda bi lecutan herfiric
Glorian ezpa yfernuyan ezta efcapaceric.

Manacendu yfernuya andi eta vortizqui
Handirenac ygoriçan luçamendu gaberic
Arima eta gorpucetan nahi tuyela icuffi
Eta emanen darayela cer vaytute mereci.

Gende honac onfa penfa iuge hunen gaynia
Nola duyen gucietan poteftate handia
Eryoan yfernuyan ceru eta lurrian
Cerendabil haren contra vada veqhatoria.

Gure artian haur dacuffat ixutarçun handia
Nola dugun cerbiçacen hanbat gure exaya
Iangoycoa defconoci gure faluaçalia
Eta oroc eçaguçen dela vide gabia.

Harren bier emanendu fentencia piçuya
Elgarrequi pena diten ifernuco garrian
Seculaco fuyan eta eceyn paufu gabian
Oroc othoy onfa penfa cerden yrabacia.

Egundano ezta içan ez içanen iagoytic

Iudicio hayn handiric ez etare vorthizich
Sortu eta forcecoac hilez guero pizturic
Oroc hara vehar dute efcufatu gaberic.

Anhiz gauça vehardira iudicio handian
Iugeac du yen poteftate parte ororen gaynian
Demandantac erran deçan vere caufa eguiaz
Bayetare defendentac bere defenfionia
Porogatu datenian norc duqueyen çucena
Sentenciaz eman deçan iugiac-nori veria.

Egun hartan iuge date mundu ororen iabia
Baytu ororen gaynian poteflate handia
Acufari vera date eta conciencia
Beqhatu oro publicoqui aguerico orduyan

Beqhatoren contra date orduyan mundu gucia
Cerenduten ofenditu hayen creaçalia
Ordu hartan ixildauque trifte veqhatoria
Orotaric cerraturic daude pauffu guciac.

Iuge iauna iraturic egonenda gaynetic
Yreftera apphaynduric yfernuya azpitic
Exay gayça acufacen ezquerreco aldetic
Beccatuyac efcuynetic minçaturen publiqui
Hire contra heben guituc ihaurrorrec eguinic
Gayzquienic contra date conciença varnetic.

Eftalceco ez içanen ehonere leqhuric

Aguercera norc eguinen ordu hartan vathiric
Mundu oro egonenda hayen contra Iarriric
Saynduac ere ordu hartan oro egonen ixilic
Iugeac ere ez ençunen ezeynereothoyc
Egun harçaz orhit guiten othoy hara gaberic.

　Nondirate egun hartan hebengo iaun erreguiac
Duque conde marques çaldun eta verce iaun nobliac
Eta hayen armadaco guiçon sendoen valentiac
ordu hartan valiaco guti hayen potenciac.

　Iurisla eta theologo poeta eta doctoriac
Procurador aduocatu iuge eta notariac
Ordu hartan aguerico clarqui hayen maliciac
Eta guti valiaco cautela eta parleriac..

　Ayta sayndu cardenale apphez eta prelatuyac
Berez eta ardi oroz eman vehar han conduya
Egun hartan handiena yçanenda erratuya
Eta vardin iuy aturen handia eta chipia.

　Aferdate egun hartan hari apellacia
Ehonere eztaçagu iaunic vere gaynian
Malicia gayci çayca eta mayte eguia
Elas othoy oroc eguin oray penitencia
Egun hartan guero eztugun eguiteco handia.

　Seynaliac ginendira aicinetic trilteric
Elementac ebiliren oro tribulaturic

　　　　　C

Iguzquia ilharguia odoletan ecinic
Ychafoa famurturic goyti eta veheyti
Hango arraynac icituric ebiliren ialguiric.

Eta lurra icigarri oro iqharaturic
çuhamu yec dacartela odolezco ycerdi
Tenpeftatez igorciriz ayre oro famurric
Mendi eta harri oro elgar çaticaturic
Mundu oro iarrirenda fu y ac arrafaturic.

Iuge iaunac manaturen vera iauguin gaberic
Gauç a oro xahu deç an vehin fu yac lehenic
Saxu eta quirax oro dohen mundu gucitic
Eta hala iarrirenda lurgucia erreric.

Trompetada minçaturen mundugucietaric
Hilac oro iayqui huna çu yen hobietaric
Arima eta gorpucetan oro vertan pizturic
Oroc hara vehar dugu efcufatu gaberic.

Iuftu oro y ganenda hertan goyti ayrian
Eta egonen efcoynetic iugearen aldean
Beccatoreac dolorezqui fugarrian lurrian
Hariqueta dançuteno fentencia gaynian.

Dagœnian gende oro aicinian vilduric
Iauguinenda rigorofqui fayndu y equi cerutic
Iofafaten egonenda airian gora iarriric
Beccatorer eguinendu arrangura handiric.

Haren hiçac eçarriren oro erdiraturic.

Hartu nahiçu yenian paſſione ſayndua
Haren contra gincenian armaturic gendia
Hiz huxbatez icituric egocitu lurrian
Iu yacera dauguinian mageſtate handian
Nola eztu loxaturen ordu hartan munduya.

Erranendu beccatorer dolorezqui orduyan
Niçaz ecineten orhit bicicinetenian
Hanbat ongui nic eguinic çuyer çuyen mendian
Eſquer honbat vqhen eztut çuy eganic vician.

Cererehon vaytuçuye oro dira eniac
Gorpuz eta hon guciac baietare arimac
çuyendaco eguin ditut lurra eta çeruyac
Iguzquia ilharguia eta fructu guciac.

Suyac vero hurac xahu hax harceco ayria
Aynguruyac çuyen goarda ararteco ſaynduyac
çuyegatic eçarridut guero neure vicia
Hoyegatic orogatic cerda çuyen paguya.

Icuſſiric anhicetan beharrian pobria
Erigoſſe egarria eta buluzcorria
Ene ycenian anhicetan galdeguinic limoſna
çuyec vqhen baytuçuye heçaz guti anſia.

Bay erhoqui conplacitu ene contra exaya

Demonio haraguia bayetare munduya
Oray dela çuyen daco maradicionia
Ifernuco fuya eta iagoytico nequia
Eta çuyen conpaynia demonio gucia.

Ezta anhiz luçaturen execucionia
Bertan date y requiren lurra oren verian
Su harequi irexiren oro vere varnian
Haur y çanen veccatoren vndar y rabacia.

Elas nola y çanenden heben damu handia
Damu handi içigarri remedio gabia
Hanbat iende feculacoz damnaturen denian
O iaun huna çuc guiçaçu othoy hantic veguira.

Veretara içuliren ditu guero veguiac
Goacen oro elgarrequi ene adifquidiac
Bethi eta feculacoz gauden ene glorian
Defir oro conplituric alegria handian.

Hantic harat ezta içanen bi erretatu bayeci
Damnatuyac ifernu y an bethi dolorerequi
Saluatuy ac ieyncoarequi bethi alegueraqui
Iangoy cuac daguiela gure partia hoyequi.

Ceruya ezta ebiliren hantic harat iagoytic
Yguzquia egonenda orienten gueldiric
Ilharguia occiden ten beguiz begui iarriric
Egun honec y raunendu eben eta iagoytic

Alabana ez içanen heben gauça viciric.

O iaun hona çucirade gure creaçalia
Beccatore baguirere oro guira çuriac
Gure faltaz gal eztadin othoy çure eguina
Beccaturic garbizaçu othoy gure arimac.

Baldin eridevten vada gutan falta handia
Are duçu handiago çutan pietatia
çuretaric guiren othoy eguiguçu gracia
çure ama anderia daquigula valia.
Oracionia
A Ve maria anderia gracia oroz bethia
Ieyncoaren ama virgen verac ordenatuya
Ceru eta lur ororen erreguina dignia
Beqhatoren aduocata eta confortaria.

Ni çugana niatorqueçu beccatore handia
Carioqui othoy cera çuçaquiztan valia
Digne ezpaniz aypacera çure ycen faynduya
Ez gitera aycinera ceren bayniz faxuya.

Mifericordiaz bethe ciren andere handia
Enaçaçula othoy yrayz eta ez menofprecia
çuc guibela badidaçu elas ama eztia
Ordu hartan diacufaçut galdu neure buruya.

Hanbat nuçu gauça orotan ni verthute gabia
Oren oroz beccatutan nabilena galduya

Etabethi erratyua nola ardi yxuya
Mundu hunec haraguiac bethi enganatuya.

çu baicira gracia ororen ama eta yturburuya
Verthute eta hon gucien theforera handia
Egundano beccatutan maculatu gabia
Verthutetan feguiçeco eguidaçu gracia.

çutan dago beccatoren remedio gucia
Sperança ofagarri eta faluamenduya
çuc guibela demaçuna nola vayta galduya
çure gomenduyan dena hala verda falbuya.

Ieyncoac çuri emandici poteftate handia
Haren ama ciren guero ama ere maytia
Ceru eta lur orotan duçun hanbat valia
Cer çuc galde baytaguiçu den conplitugucia.

Eta çure efcutic duten verce oroc gracia
Eta falua çuc deçaçun çuri gomendatuya
O andere excelente eceyn pare gabia
Saluatu yetaric niçan eguidaçu gracia.

çuri gomendacen nuçu hila eta vicia
Neure gorpuz eta arima eta dudan gucia
Othoy vehar orduyetan çuçaquiçat valia
Eta othoy çuc goberna ene vici gucia.

Eta yrabaz ieyncoaganic indar eta gracia

Beccatuyez eguiteco vnſa penitencia
Eta guero verthutet an deramadan vicia
Eta eguin gauç a orotan haren vorondatia.

Beguira othoy meſcabutic ene gorpuz pobria
Beccatutan hil eznadin eguidaçu gracia
Seculacos damnaturic enoyan galduya
Bana çure eſcutic dudan ſaluaceco vidia.

Eta guero dauguinian ene eryocia
Arimaren particeco oren ycigarria
Ordu hartan behar baytut eman condu herſia
Eguin oroz recebitu neure merexituya.

Eta ez iaquin lehen gaoyan nondaten oſtatuya
Ez etare çu ezpacira nordaquidan valia
Ordu hartan helç aquiçat othoy ama eztia
Ararteco leyal eta neure ayutaria.

Othoy çure gomenduyan har arima triſtia
Ordu hartan io ezteçan yfernuco vidia
çure feme iaunarequi eguidaçu baquia
Beccatuyac barqhaturic didan parabiçuya.

Eta nic handacuſadan çure veguitartia
Eta ſaynduyequi lauda haren mageſtatia
çeren vnſa orhit citen niçaz ama eztia
Gogo honez erranendut çuri aue maria.

Oracione haur derrana andredona maria
Othoy gomendatu duçun hila eta vicia.

¶ Amorofen gaztiguy a

Bercec berceric gogoan eta nic andredona maria
Andre hona daquigula gucior othoy valia.

Amorofac nahi nuque honat veha valite
Honliçaten gaztiguric aguian enzun liroyte
Amorebat haut aceco confey lubat neque ye
Balinetan feculacoz gogoan far valequie.

Ni haurc ere vqhen dicit ceynbaytere amore
Bana hantic eztut vqhen prouechuric batere
Anhiz pena arima gal hanera eta neuryere
Amoretan plazer baten mila dira dolore.

Amoretan othed ate ley aldenic batere
Hiz ederrez ezpa ioy az mutha eztadin huraere
Hoben vfte du yenori anhicetan traydore
Hobena date gay zenic arimaren berere

Beqhatuzco amoria bethi date traydore
Erioa dauguinian eguia çogueridate
Hartuduten plazer oro orduy an y ragand ate
Beccatuy a gueldicenda penaçeco guero ere
Anhiz plazer vqhen badu anhiz vehardolore.

Amorebat nahi nuque liadutanic eguia
Vici eta hilez guero hayn laquidan valia
Cerbiçatu nahi nuque halacoa vician
Heben labur viciada iagoyticoz bercia.

Mundu oro iraganic ez eriden berceric
Ieyncqaren ama hona gracia oroz betheric
Haren amore içateco ezta ehor digneric
Vnsa cerbiça daçagun mayte guitu bertaric.

Amoriac vano dira harçaz berceguciac
Behar handiendenian faltaturen berciac
Vfte bano lehenguira hilcen beqhatoriac
Harc ayuta ezpaguiça nola guiren galduyac.

Andre hona hardaçagun oroc gure amore
Berce oro vci eta eguin hariohore
Hala eguin vadaçagu ohoratu guirate
Berce gatic hura gabe oro galdu guirade.

Ieyncoaz landan mundu oroc eztu hanbat valia
Ceruya lurra ychaffoa haren peco gucia
Oro tara hedacendu vehar vada efcuya
Bera handi içan arren preciacen chipia
Halacoa vci eta nonduquegu bercia.

Berce amoreac baten veci eztirade pereftu
Norc beria berciari eztu nahi partitu
Ama virgen gloriofa hanbat vada conplitu

D

Ororençat bera bayta ley aldela abaſtu.

Amoroſec bad aguite vehin bere nahia
Handiago gitençaye berce nahicaria
Eci vqhen behinere bere conplimenduya
Bethi peytu deramate bere mende gucia
Emazte eta guiçonoroc har amore maria
Eta orori vaytequegu berac conplimenduya.

Andre honac vqhen dici ederretan gracia
Ehorc hura gayxteriaz ecin leçan inbia
Bana viſtaz hilcençuyen nahicari ſaxuya
Figuraren eqhuſtiaz daquiqueçu eguia.

Ychaſſoan hur gucia ceruyetan içarra
Oyhanetan içalori lurgucian velharra
Egunarı yguzquiagau belçari ilhuna
Lehen faltaturen dira eci hura gugana
Balinetan eguiazqui gubagaude hargana.

Cerenbadaerho guira gayxo beqhatariac
Andre ley al honegana goacen othoy guciac
Elas othoy aribira berce amore falſuyac
Harequila ſegur dugu vehar dugun gucia.

Elas amoros gaixoa hire enganatuya
Erhogoatan badaramac eure mende gucia
Ene andere graciofa ezpad aquic valia
Bay bician bay hilian bethi oha galduya.

Dembora duyan artian eguic ahal honguia
Eryoa danguinian miraz duquec orduya
Orduyan ere nahi vaduc onfa ialguidaguia
Onfa harigomendadi nic dioffat eguia
Finianere eztic vzten harc galcera veria
Orduyan ere vere efcuyan dic gracia gucia.

Mundu honec anhiz gende enganatu darama
Iagoyticoz vici vftez haren fehidabilça
Guti vfte duyenian ehor vci darama
Erho ioqhatuyadate hartan fidadadina.

Ni haur ere ebiliniz anhicetan erhoric
Gaoaz eta egunaz ere hoçic eta veroric
Loa galdu pena afqui bana ez arimagatic
Oray oro nahi nuque liren ieyncoagatic.

*Nibeçala anhiz duçu halacoric munduyan
Mende oro dohatenic bethi vana glorian
Ohart guiten buruyaridenboraden artian
Andre honac harguiçaque gomendutan aguian
Hanbat bada graciofa ama ororen gaynian
Gindadinic eztu vzten hartu gabe gracian

Culpa gabe ehor ezta haurda fegureguia
Beqhatuyaz damnacendu iangoycoac munduya
Beqhaturic ezta yçan çutan andre handia
Ararteco çaquizculadigun varqhamenduya.

Beccatoren faluaceco ieyncoac eguin cinducen
Bere buruy a eguin dici iuge iufticiaren
çu mifericordiaren refugio cinaden
Nola berac iuftician ecin falualiçaque
çure mifericordiaz remedia litecen
Balinetan eguiazqui çugana gin valite.

Egundano ezta yçan ez içanen iagoytic
Beqhatore hay nandiric ez etare faxuric
Berebidian iauguin vada çuri gomendaturic
Vqhen eztuyen barqhamendu çure amorecatic
Ez galduda ez galduren çure gomenducoric
çuri gomendacen guira hilic eta viciric.

Berce emaztiac ama dira cenbayt haurto chipiren
Eta guero obororic puncela ecin dirate
çu anderia ama cira virginaric ieyncoaren
Eta gueroz erreguina ceru eta lurraren.

Ieyncoa iaunden gauça ororen çu cirade andere
Arrazoynda mundu oroc daguien çuri ohore
Eci halafariçaucu lhefu chriſto vera ere
çuc beçanbat dignitate mundu oroc eztuque.

O anderia ecin date ehor çure vardinic
Gaynecoric çuc eztuçu ieynco veraz berceric
Ieynco ezten verce oro dago çure azpitic
Ieyncoaren ama cira mundu oroz gay netic.

Mundu oroc eztu eguin çuc beçanbat hargatic
Orogatic bano oboro harc ere daydi çugatic
Bere ama ecin vci obeditu gaberic
Othoy gracia eguiguçu guiren çu yenetaric.

Vnſa çuc harbanençaçu gomendutan gogotic
Ecin damna nayndeyela cineſtendut ſegurqui
Anhiz veguiratu duçu galduren cenetaric
Niri ere hel ç aquiç at othoy galdu gaberic.

Ehonere gay zrc ezta çuc qhen eztiroçunic
Ez etare hontaſſunic çure eſcuy an eztenic
Denbora eta leqhu orotan ecyn duda gaberic
Graciac oro çure eſcuyan iangoycoac emanic.

Nahi duyena hala duque amac ſemiaganic
Seme honaç anhiz daydi amaren amorecatic
Gure natura haritudu çutan amoraturic
Iangoycoa ezarri duçu gure anayeturic.

Haren eta gure ororen ama cira digneric
Amac eztu ſofriceco ſemen artian guerlaric
Samurturic badacuxu gure gaizqui egatic
Ororen ama cira eta baqueguiçaçu bertaric.

Oray eguiten diraden gayzqui handi egatic
Ieyncoac ondatu çuqueyen lur gucia engoytic
Balinetan çu ezpacina ararteco gugatic
Oro ſoſtengacen guitu çure othoyegatic

Gu gayxtoac içan arren ezten çutan faltaric
Fin honera helguiçaçu guiren falbuyetaric.

Ama eztia nic badaguit çure contra faltaric
çuc gaztiga eta dreça naç açu othoy bertaric
Elas norat ihes naydi çu neure ama vciric
Neuretaco eztaçagut çu nolaco amaric.

❡Emazten fauore:

Emaztiac ez gayz erran ene amorecatic
Guiçonec vci valiç ate elaydite faltaric.

Anhiz guiçon ari bada andrez gayzqui errayten
Arhizqui eta defonefqui baytituzte aypacen
Yxilica egoytia eder rago liçate
Andrec guiçonequi beci huxic ecin daydite.

çuhur gutic andre gatic gayzqui erran diroyte
Hayez hongui erraytea oneftago liçate
Emazteac cerengatic gaiz erranendirate
Handi eta chipi oro hayetaric guirade.

Balentia finpleada andren gayz erraytea
Bat gayz erran nahi vadu oro vardin farcea
Yxil ladin nahi nuque halacoden gucia
Damugaycic emazteac hari eman dithia

Andren gayz errayle oroc bearluque penfatu

Bera eta verce oro nontic guinaden forthu
Ama emazte luyen ala ez nahi nuque galdatu
Amagatic andre oro beharluque goratu

Guiçonaren prouechuco emaztia bethi da
Oro behin hayetaric forcen guira mundura
Sorthu eta hilguinate harc haz ezpaguiniça
Haciz guero egun oroz behar haren ayuta.

Haren efcuz offoan behar foynera eta iatera
Eridenian andre gabe galdu guiçon egurra
Hil badadi hura nola nordoaque gaynera
Ordu oroz behartugu ezta heben cerduda

Emazteric ezten lecuyan eztacufat plazeric
Ez guiçona ez echia behinere x ahuric
Echianden gauça oro gayzqui erreglaturic
Parabiçuyan nahi enuque emazteric ezpaliz.

Emaztiac eztut ençun lehen guiçona iauquiric
Bana guiçonac emaztia bethiere lehenic
Gayxteria ialguitenda bethi guiçonetaric
Ceren hada daraucate emaztiari hoguenic.

Bertuteac veharluque guiçonetan handiago
Emaztetan nic dacuffat honguiz ere guehiago
Mila guiçon gazxtoric da emaztebatendaco
Guiçon baten mila andre bere fedean dago.

Hec guiçoner veha valite eliçate bat honic
Eztirovte deufc aydenic vci iauqui gaberic
Bana anhiz emazteda efcapacen çayenic
Anderetan ceren bayta vertutea hobenic.

Nic eztançut emaztiac borchaturic guiçona
Banavera çoratutic andriaridarrayca
Cenbayt andre hel baledi oneriztez hargana
Ceyn guiçonec andriari emaytendu oguena.

Ieyncoac emaztea mayte mundu oroz gaynetic
Cerutica iayxicedin harçaz amoraturic
Emaztiac eçarridu gure anayeturic
Andre oro laudaceco haren amorecatic.

Irudiçayt emaztia dela gauça eztia
Donario gucietan guciz gauça emya
Gaoaz eta egunaz ere badu plazer handia
Harçaz gayzqui erraytia vilania handia.

Munduyan ezta gauçaric hayn eder ez placentic
Nola emaztia guiçonaren petic buluzcorriric
Beffo viac ç abalduric dago errendaturic
Guiçonorrec daguiela harçaz nahiduyenic.

Iobadeça dardoaz ere gorpuzaren erditic
Aynguruyac banooboro ezlarraque gayzquiric
Banadardoaematuric çauriere fendoturic
Bere graciaz ezarteyntu elgarrequi vaqueturic.

Norda guiçon modorroa harçaz orhit eztena
Eta guero halacoa gayzerrayten duyena
Ezta guiçon naturazco hala eguiten duyena
Ceren eztu eçagucen hala hongui eguina.

¶Ezconduyen coplac

Iangoycoa edetaçu vercerena gogotic
Bera captiuada eta ni gathibu hargatic.

Ni gathibu naducana captiuada bercereu
Ene dichac hala eguindu ny gathibu bigaren
Gogo honez içaneniz vicy baniz bataren
Bana borchaz bayecila ez iagoytic verciaren.

Bercerena hardaçanac beretaco amore
Qborotan vqhenendu plazer bano dolore
Baçarriac veqhan eta veldurrequi dirate
Guti vſte dutenian gayça bertan ſordayte.

Honeſtea bercerena erhogoa handida
Plazer vaten vqhenendu anhiz malenconia
Beguyez icus eein minça handacuſat nequia
Bery arequi daçanian enetaco aycia.

Perilequi bayecila ecin noaque hargana
Eta aguian harc orduyan ezpaytuque aycina
Baduere veldur date vertan doha harçara
Nic nahyen dudanian bercech bѐſſoan daraça.

E

Alhor hartan helbadaquit ereytèra hacia
Eta ene vada ere laſtoa eta vihia
Ez bat ori ahalduquet ezetare vercia
Lan eguinaz eſquer gayxto galdu y rabacia
Bercerenzat gueldicenda ene çucenbidia
Aguyan guero alabarequi ez conduco femya.

Amoria ehorc ere eztu nahi partitu
Nic eztaquit berciac vana ny aryniz beqhatu
Beriarequi eqhuſtiaz hayn hay n noha penatu
Hec doſtetan ni nequetan orduyan errabiatu

Geloſiac eztiçaquet nic gayz erran feculan
Mayte nuyena nahi enuque ehorc hunquiliaçadan
Bercerenaz yçanuçu amoros leqhu batetan
Beriagana geloſturic defeſperacer ninz an

Amoria ecyn cençuz ecin dayte goberna
Anhicetan honeſtendu guti vehar duyena
Arnoac vano gayzqui ago ordidiro perſona
Sarri eſtaca berant lacha harc hazeman deçana

Amoria ixuda eta eztaçagu çucena
Eztu vſte berceric dela lecot mayte duyena
Suyac vano gayzquiago erradiro guicona
Xchaſſoac ez yraungui erachequi dadina.

❡ Amoros fecretugui dena

Andre eder gentilbatec vihoça der aut ebaxi
Harçaz orhit nadinian deufere ecin yrexi
Nic hura nola nahi nuque harc banença onhexi
Ecin venturatuz nago beldur daquion gayci.

Miray lbat nic ahalbanu hala luyen donoa
Neure gogoa neracuxon fecretuqui han varna
Han veryan nic nacuffen harena ere nigana
Huxic ecin eguin neçan behinere hargana.

Ene gayzqui penaceco hayn ederric fortucen
Gaoaz eta egunaz ere gayzqui nici penacen
Harequila bat banadi vihoçazayt harricen
Neure penen erraytera are eniz aufarcen.

Enegogoa balyaqui mayte vide nynduque
Nierregue valinbaninz erreguina liçate
Hura hala nahi valiz elgarrequi guinate
Haren haurrac eta eniac aurride offo lirate.

Valinetan nic vanerro hari neure vihoça
Eta guero valinbalit refpuefta bortiça
Dardoac vano lehen liro erdira ene vihoça
Duda gabe eror naynde han berian hilhoça

Artiçarrac bercetaric abantailla darama
Hala verda anderetan ni penacen nuyena
Hanbat da eder eta gentil harçaz erho narama
çori honian fortu date haren beffoan daçana.

Ene gogoa nola vayta çucen iarri hargana
Harenere iangoycoac dacarrela nygana
Ene pena faïdaquion vihocian varrena
Gogo hunez eguin daçan defiracen dudana

¶ Amorofen partizia

Parti albanenguidio harc ezluque pareric
Ala vana nic ezticit hayn honderiçadanic.

Amorebat onhexidut guciz foberatuqui
Ene arima eta vihoça iollidira harequi
Haren y rudi ederrori veguietan ehoqui
Harçaz orhit nadiniah vihoza doat ebaqui.

Nic hargana hanbat dicit amoryo handia
Harequila egoytiaz ezpaneynde enoya
Harganico particia ene eyhar garria
Berriz icus dirodano bethi malenconia.

Elas ene amoria nola nuçun penacen
çurequila ecin vathuz vihocian erracen
Ene gaizqui penacecofegur forthu cinaden
Penac oro honlirate çu bacina orhicen.

Minzaceco çurequila gaubat nahi niqueci
Hilabete conplituric hura luça valedi
Arranguren qhondaceco afti nuyen frangoqui
Eceynere veldurgabe egoyteco çurequi.

Oray porogacen dicit daquitenen errana
Ehorc vci eztaçala efcu y etan du yena
Elas yzul albaneça y raganden denbora
Segur oray enyqueci dudan gogoan veharra

Denbora hartan ohinicin nic çugatic dolore
Oray aldiz çure faltaz muthatuniz ny ere
Malencony a ecitela vaduqheçu amore
Bana ordu vacinduque cençaceco çuc ere.

Badaquiçu dolory an partaydenyz ny ere
Eta çure muthaceco ez oguenic batere
Neure gay zqui penaceeo harcinçadan amore
Iagoyticoz vqhenendut nic çugatic dolore.

¶ Amoros gelofia

Beti penaz yçatia gay zda ene amore
Beti ere vehardura nic çugatic dolore.

Amorebat vqhendicit miragarri gentilic
Harequila ninçanian enu yen nic faltaric
Nic iagoytic ecyn nuque hura veçayn mayteric
Haren minez oray nago ecin hilez viciric.

Norc baytere amoria niri daraut muthatu
Nic eztaquit cerden vana eftamendu verridu
Ohi nola afpaldian nahi eçayt minçatu
Çerq andere han tuduyen vehardicit galdatu.

Secretuqui vehardicit harequila minçatu
Ordu hartan iagoyticoz'exay ezpa vaquetu
Nyri vnfa ezpadaguit vehardicit pintatu
Ene buruya ciaydaçu harendaco abaftu.

Amoria nor yç anda gure bion artian
Muthaturic vaçabilça ia afpaldi handian
Nic çugana d aquidala faltatu eztut vician
Bioc behin fecretuqui nonbait mynça guitian.

Ehonere eztacuffat nihaur veçayn erhoric
Nic norgatic pena vaytut harc ene eztu axolic
çuhur banynz banynçande ny ere hura gaberic
Alabana ecin vci vehin ere gogotic.

Gende honac vihoça daut bethiere nygarrez
Neure amore chotiltua galdu dudan veldurrez
Gaoaz loric ecin daydit haren gogoan veharrez
Gogoan vehar handidicit bethe nnyen adarrez.

Iangoycoa edetaçu amoria gogotic
Eta haren yrudia ene veguietaric
Harc nigana eztaduca vnfa ley aldateric
Ni ere elicaturenyz oray hura gaberic
Saroyada lohitu eta eztut haren veharric
Nahi badut vqhenendut oray ere berriric.

¶Potaren galdacia

Andria ieyncoac drugaçula oray verdi guirade
Ny erregue balinbanynz erreguinacinate
Potbat othoy eguidaçu ezayçula herabe
Nic çugatic dudan penec hura merexidute.

Eya horrat apartadi nor vſtedüc niçala
Horlacobat eztuc vſte nyc icuſſidudala
Horrelaco hiz gaixtoric niry eztarradala
Vercer erran albaytiça enuc vſte duyana

Andre gaixtoa bacinade nic eznaydi conduric
Ciren cirena baycira çuçaz penadicit nic
Ene vſtian eztut erran deſoneſtaden gauçaric
Potbat niri eguinagatic ecinduque laydoric,

Hire potac bacyaquyat berce gauça nahidic
Anderia azticira nihaurc erran gaberic
Bada vci albaynençac ny holacoz yxilic
Horreyn gayz ciraden guero eguinendut verceric.

Vicinyçan egunetan vada ecitut vciren
Nic ceroray nahi vaytut heben duçu eguinen
Vſtediat eſcuy arqui eciçala burlacen
Guiçon hunec oray nuya heben laydoz veteren
Eyagora nyccer daydit çauden yxilic hanbaten.

Etay lelo rybay lelo pota franco vercia vego
Andria minça albaycinde verce aldian emiago.

¶Amorez errequericia

B Enedica fortuna ala encontru hona
Oray beguietan dicit defiracen nuyena.

Ene mayte maytenaeguidaçu çucena
Ioanduçuna eqhardaçu ezpa eman ordayna

Nicdaquidan gauçaric eztaducat çureric
Loxaturic iarri nuçu ezpaytaquit cegatic.

Eztuçula veldurric eztuqueçu perylic
Gure aucian ezta yçanen çu haurbeci iuyeric.

Eztut eguyn gayzquiric vqheyteco perilic
Ez etare ceren gatic vehar dudan auciric.

Vada neure maytia nic dioxut eguia
Arrobatu nuçu eta valia vequit neurya.

Ny enuçu ohoyna arrobaçer nyçana.
Oray othoy enadila oguen gabedifama.

Enetaco ohoyn cira ohoyn ere handicira
Nic veharren nuyen gauça daramaçu çurequila.

Ni enuçu iaquinxu clarqui erran eçaçu
Ehorc vnfa adi ciçan nahi valin baduçu.

Guiçonac duyen maytena bay etare hobena
Vihoceco paufuya du eta vere lo huna.

Oray loric ecin daydit vihocian ezpaufuric
Hayec biac galdu ditut amoria nic çugatic.

Vnfa penfa vadeçaçu gayzqui arrobatunuçu
çor handian çaude eta othoy vnfa eguydaçu.

Galdu valin baditnçu ceren oguen derautaçu
Nic daquidan leqhutaric ni baytara eztituçu.

Oray egun vatetan cenaudela penfetan
Hanbat çuçaz amoratu gueroz nuçu penatan.

Horla erraytia errax duçu erho bocen vadaquiçu
çura pena dioçunoc nonbayt handi videytuçu.

Hanbatere handi tuçu ecin erran nizaqueçu
Eguiara vaciniaqui vrricari nanguidiçu.

Penac handi vadituçu acheterric afquiduçu
Sarri fendoturen cira larruyori offoduçu.

çauri banynz larruyan vada acheter herrian
Ene mina fendo ezliro çuc bayeci vician.

çure yrudi ederrac eta mayna gentilac
Gayzquiago çauri nici ecidardo çorroçac.

F

.Vihocian çauri nuçu eta gathibatu nuçu
Amoretan harnaçaçu nic dudana çureduçu.

Amexetan aguerritan ni çugatic doloretan
Hizbat honic erradaçu hil eznadin othoy bertan.

Cer nahiduçu darradan gauça horren gaynian.
Mi nolacoric afqui duçu berceric ere herrian.

Verce oroz gaynetic hanbat mayte citut nic
Mundu oro vzi niro çure amorecatic.

Albañerra eguya nyc dut pena handia
Secretuqui minça guiten bioc othoy maytia.

¶ Amorofen difputa

Vztaçu hurrancera amore mayte
Oray particeco damu guiniate.

Amoryac othoy partiguitecen
Gendiac diradela haffi beqhaicen
Laydoc hartu gabe gueldi guitecen
Gendec yrrigarri guerta ezquiten.

Elas amoriaene galduya
Iamas çurequila enaynde enoya
Biciric particia pena handia
Honeyn farri vci nahi nuçuya.

Ni haurc ere guerthúz mayte bacitut
Onerizte gabez vzten eçitut
Vana ieyncoaren nuçu beldurtu
Sobera diguici eguyı beqhatu.

Orano amorea gazte guituçu
Ieyncuaz orhiceco leqhu diguçu
Are elgarrequi vehar diguçu
Oray particeco damu guituçu.

Beccatu honetan hilenbaguina
Damnatuluqueçu ene arıma
Ecitela engoytic nıtan engaña
Nyri phoroguric eztidaçula.

Cineftebat dicit gogoan honela
Nic nola daducat amore çugana
Ieyntoariere edet çaycala
Hargatıc gaycexi ezquiçaquela.

Horlaco laufenguz vci naçaçu
Nola erhoturic narabilaçu
Othoy ceniçauçu nyry euztaçu
Ene gogoa vnfa eztacufaçu.

Nola dioftaçu horlaco hiça
Bethi daducaçu tema borthiça
Ioandaraudaçu lehen vihoça
Guero gathibatu neure gorpuça

Horlaceco erançutez vci naçaçu
Gueldi vacinite nahi nv queçu
Gure echian ohart vadaquizquigu
Bioc iagoyticos galdu guituçu.

Gendiac fo daudia bethi gugana
Ni haurc fecretuqui.nator çuganⁱ
çu haurc daquiqueçu noyzden ayzyna
Neque eçayçula gitia nigana.

Picher ebilia hauxi diohaçu
çuc ny laydo handiz vetheren nuçu
Othoy cenyçayçu ny ri vztaçu
Niçaz axeguinic ecinduqueçu.

Amore maytia dioxut eguia
çutan diagoçu ene vicia
Nahiago dicit çure iqhuftia
Eci neuretaco herri gucia.

Horlaco laufenguz vci naçaçu
Ichil vacinite nahi niqueçu
Ieyncoaz orhiceco ordu luqueçu
Berceric har eçaçu niri vztaçu.

Ieynco veldurturic iarriciraya
Halaz defpeditu nahi.nuçuya
Hebetic ioan gabe ene buruya
Eguin vehar duçu ene nahia.

Oray ñahinuçuya heben vorchatu
Aldihonetan othoy vci naçaçu
Berce aldibatez ginen ñyçayçu
Nahiduçun ori orduyan daydiçu.

Haraycinacoric duçu errana
Vcidaçanorrec efcuyan duyena
Nahiduyenian eztuqueyela
Hiçac haribira dugun eguyna.

Oray eguynduçu nahiduçuna
Emandarautaçu ahalgueyçuna
Maradi cacendut neure fortuna
Ceren gin vaynendin egun çugana.

Amore ecitela othoy defpara
Honat veguitartez yçul çaquiçat
Nivaytanduqueçu adifquidebat
Valia diquecit feñhar gayxtobat.

¶Ordu gayçarequi horrat zaquiçat

Oray vehar dnguya conquifta verri
Eztey yraganez gomitu handy
Hanbat ecirade andere larri
Merexi duçuna narçaque farri.

¶Amore gogorraren defpita.

Andre eder gentilbatez hautatuç ayt veguia
Herri orotan gauça oroz eztu vere paria
Othoy cebat banegu yon larradala eguia
Biderican liç atenez nynzan haren gracian

Refpoftu ya emanderaut luç amendu gaberic
Cortefiaz honderiçut nic çuri hayn fegurqui
Berceric nitan eztuqueçu abifacencitut nic
Gazte çoroa nyçan arren enuqueçu hargatic.

çugaztia bacirere adi mendu hon duçu
Nic çugatic dudan pena othoy fendieçaçu
çure taco harnazaçu vici nahi vanuçu
Ni çu gatic hil banadi cargu handi duqueçu.

Ohoria galcendela plazerguitia gayzduçu
Niri horla erraytia çuri eman eztuçu
Gayxteria eguitia laydodela daquiçu
Ny erhoa çu iaqu ynxu veha enaquidiçu.

çuhaur nahi bacirade ni fegretu nuqueçu
Gure arteco amoria ehorc eciaquiqueçu
Secretuqui minça:eco othoy bide ydaçu
Enequila minçaciaz gayçiq ecin duqueçu.

Gayzqui eguind adinian gendec farri daquite
Ene gayzqui eguitiaz enec laydo luqueyte
çu eta ni elgarrequi vnfa ecin guynate
çaude yxilic çoaz horrat eta hobe baitate.

Hiz horreçaz erdiratu deraudaçn viboça
Nic çugatic dudan pena hanbat ere handida
çuçaz veraz ezpanadi oray vertan confola
Ene arima ialguirenda falta gabe canpora.

Arimaren ialguitia neque handiaduçn
Oray duçun penegatic çuria egonenduçu
Horrelaco vanitatez nyrifegur vztaçu
Prouechuric eztuqueçu eta cinhez nazaçu.

çurequila gayzqui vaniz nola viciminçande
Ene vihoz eta aruna çurequila dirade
Vihoz eta arima gabe ehor ecin liçate
çu eta ni elgarrequi vnfa ahalguinate

Iauna guerthuz hic daducat porfidia handia
Ixil endin nahi niquec ala ene fedia
Hiz gutitan adi ezac nahi vaduc eguia
Hiretaco eztiaducat guerthuz neure buruya.

Hori horla liçatela nicin neure veldurra
Andriac honderiçanari ezpadaqui mefura
Ni lehenic eta guero amoros oro galduda
Nic çuri hon vaderiçut gayzci eztaquiçula

Egundano yçan daya ni baydichatacoric
Ny amoriac enu mayte nic hura ecin gaycexi
Vfte dicit narrayola ecin duquedanari
Ceren vada hon derizat hon ezteriztanari.

Iangoycoa mutha ez:ic othoy ene vihoça
Amoriaren harc veçala nic eztudan axola
Borchaz ere gavzqui bano hongui eguitia hobeda
Ni haurc ere vcirendut hon ezteriztadana.

Andre faltaz eniz hilen valinba ni lehena
Orozexi vehardicit non vaytate hobena
Hequi ecin medra nayte bay gal neure arima
Bategatic farri niro diren oroz arnega.

Moſſen Bernat echaparere cantu ya

Moſſen bernat iaquin vahu gauça nola ginencen
Bearnora gabetaric egon ahal inçanden.

Heldu veharduyen gauçan ezta efcapaceric
Nic oguenic eznu yela hongui guitez verceric
Bide gabec haritunu vide eznuyen leqhutic
Erregueri gayzqui faldu guertuz oguengaberic.

Iaun erreguec meçu nenzan ioanenguion bertaric
Gaycez lagola ençun nuyen bana nicez oguenic
Izterbeguier eneyen malician leqhuric
Ioan nendin enaguien oguen gabe ihe fic.

Valinetan ioan ezpaninz oguenduru ninçaten
Ene contra falferia bethi cinhexi çaten
Iuſtician ençun vaninz farri ialgui ninçaten
Haren faltaz haſſi nuçu iauguiriaz dolucen.

Vercen gayçaz cençacia çuhurcia handida
Izterbegui duyen oro nitan vedi gaztiga
Abantallan dabilela albay ledi fegura
Gayça apart egoy ztea bethiere hobeda.

Ni gayxoa exayari ni haur giniz efcura
Ene vnfa eguinac ere oray oro gay zdira
Haren menian ezpanengo nic nuqueyen çucena
Miraculu vanagui ere oray ene oguena.

Falfu teftimoniotic ecin ehor veguira
Halaz condemnatu çuten ieyncoa erehilcera
Beccatore guira eta mira eztaquigula
Balinetan vide gabe acufatu baguira
Paciença dugun eta ieyncoac guizan ayuta
Malician dabilena verac diro mendeca.

Iangoycua çucirade eguiazco iugia
çure gortean vardindira handi eta chipia
Norc vaytere eguyn deraut malicia handia
Hayer hura othoy barqha niri valia eguia.

Iangoycoa çuc veguira exayaren menetic
Nic eniac badacufquit ene gayçaz vozturic
çure efcuyaz dacufquidan heyec gaztigaturic
Ene gaynian eztaguiten vfteduten yrriric.

Iangoycua eguin dicit çure contra beccatu
Hayez nahienuçula othoy heben punitu

G

Erreguéri daquid ala nic ezticit faltatu
Ceren egon vehardud an heben hanbat gatibu.

çuganaco huxeguinez nahi banuçu punitu
Erregue eta verce oro ene contra armatu
Gogo honez nahi dicit çure eguina laudatu
Eta exayac didan pena pacientqui haritu
Nahiz heben pena nadin arimaden faluatu
Hayec cer merexiduten çuhaurorrec iqhuftzu.

Penac oro gitendira ieyncoaren nahitic
Eta verac permiticen oro hobenagatic
Aguian hula ezpanango hil ninçanden engoytic
Ene exayac galdu vftian ene horla eguindic.

Berac baçu hil dirade ni are nago viciric
Hongui eguin vfte vaytut ohorezqui ialguiric
Gayça nola hona ere iauguinenda vertaric
Gayz eqhuffi eztu yenaç hona çerden eztaqui.

Hongui eguitez gayz fofrituz vehardugu faluatu
Pena eta miferia nic enuyen daftatu
Oray daquit iango ycuac enu nahi damnatu
Heben ene penacera çaydan yan orhitu
Vrhe hunac vehardici fuy an vnfa purgatu.

Vere nahi ezpanindu eninduquen punitu
Aytac vere haur maytia gaztigatu ohidu
Bihi hunac gorde gabe vehardici xahutu

Iangoycoac nizaz ere hala aguian eguindu.

Moſſen bernat penſa ezac carcel hori gayzbada
Non baytere yfernuya are gayçago dela
Heben hic vaduquec vana hayecez norc conſola
Penac heben findic ſarrihayenac ez ſeculan.

Vatre minic heben eztuc lecot ialgui nahia
Handirenec bethidie ſuyan pena handia
Pena handi ycigarri eceyn pauſu gabia
Harçaz orhit adi eta duquec paciencia.

Vercen gaztigari inçan oray adi gaztiga
Pena honez orhit eta hangoa ezac cogita
Hebengoaz vercecoa albaheça eſcuſa
Vnſa enplegatu duquec heben eure denbora.

Hor balego gaztigay ro ihaurc verce gucia
Bada oray gaztiguezac aldiz eure burya
Quiry ſayluy ari nola hiri hel eztaquia
Bercer argui eguin eta erracendic buruya.

Hiri eguin vadaraye bide gabe handia
Ieyncoari gomendezac eure gauça gucia
Harc orori emanendic bere merexituya
Gayzqui guiler pena handi pacienter gloria.

Eztaçala gayzeriztez damna heure buruya
deſiratuz gayxtoari hel daquion gayzquia

Ieyncuari eguitenduc in iuria handia
Hura borrer eguitenduc iuge eure buruya.

Certan iuya hic vaytaçac eure yzterbeguia
Hartan condemnacenduquec yhaurc eure buruya
Eta hartan eztaquidic efcufaric valia
Eracuftac ehonere norden oguen gabia.

Iangoycua oray dicit eguiteco handia
Hiri honetan eryocez hilcenduçu gendia
Gathi butan hil enadin guiçon oguen gabia
Offoric othoy ialguiteco çuc ydaçu vidia
Izterbeguiac eztaguidan guibeletic irria
Oguenduru çuyan eta hangaldudic vicia.

Libertatia nola vayta gaucetaco hobena
Gathi butan egoytia hala pena gaycena
Ny veçala eztadila othoy ehor engana
Ez etare hiz orotan fida ere guiçona
Iaygoycua çuc veguira niri ere çucena.

Amen.

Contrapas

Heufcara ialgui adi cápora

Garacico herria
Benedicadadila
Heufcarari emandio
Behardu yen thornuya.

Heufcara
Ialgui adiplaçara

Berce gendec vfteçuten
Ecin fcriba çayteyen
Oray dute phorogatu
Euganatu cirela.

Heufcara
Ialgui adi mundura

Lengoagetan ohi inçan
Eftimatze gutitan
Oray aldiz hic beharduc
Ohoria orotan.

Heufcara
Habil mundu gucira

Berceac oroc içan dira
Bere goihen gradora
Oray hura iganenda
Berce ororen gaynera.

Heufcara

Bafcoac oroc preciatzē
Heufcaraez iaquin harrē
Oroc iccaffiren dute
Oray cerden heufcara.

Heufcara

Oray dano egon bahiz
Imprimitu bagueric
Hi engoitic ebiliren
Mundu gucietaric.

Heufcara

Eceyn erelengoageric
Ez francefa ez berceric
Oray eztaerideyten
Heufcararen pareric.

Heufcara
Ialgui adi dançara.

¶Sautrela
Heuſcara da campora, eta goacen oro dançara

O heuſcara laude ezac garacico herria
Ceren hantic vq̃hen baytuc behardu yan thornu ya
Lehenago hi baitinçan lengoagetan azquena
Oray aldiz içaneniz orotaco lehena.

Heuſcaldunac mundu orotan preciatu ciraden
Bana hay en lengoagiaz berceoro burlatzen
Ceren eceyn ſcripturan erideiten ezpaitzen
Oray dute iccaſſiren nolagauça honacen.

Heuſcaldun den guiçon oroc alcha beça buruya
Eci huyen lengoagia içanenda floria
Prince eta iaun handiec oroc haren galdia
Scribatus halbalute iqhaſteco deſira.

Deſir hura conplitu du garacico naturac
Eta haren adifquide oray bordelen denac
Lehen imprimiçalia heuſcararen hurada
Baſco oro obligatu iagoiticoz hargana

Etay lelori bailelo leloa çaray leloa
Heuſcara da campora eta goacen oro dançara.

DEBILE PRINCIPIVM MELIOR
FORTVNA SEQVATVR.

¶Extraiĉt des regeſtes de Parlement.

Vpplie humblement Françoys Mor-
pain, maiſtre Imprimeur de ceſte ville
de Bourdeaulx, que pour imprimer vn
petit traĉte intitule, Linguæ vaſconum
primitie, luy a conuenu faire pluſieurs
fraiz & miſes. A ceſte cauſe plaiſe a la
Court inhibitions eſtre faiĉtes a tous les Imprimeurs
libraires de ce Reſſort de imprimer ou faire imprimer
lediĉt Traĉte, & a tous marchãs de nen vendre d autre
impreſſion dans troys ans a peine de mil liures tourñ.
& ferez iuſtice. Veue laquelle requeſte la court faiĉt les
inhibitions requiſes par lediĉt Morpain a peine de mil
liures tourñ. Faiĉt a Bourdeaulx en Parlement le dernier iour Dapuril, mil cinq cens quarante cinq.
Collation eſt faiĉte.

De Pontac.

Linguæ Vasconum Primitiæ

The First Fruits of the Basque Language, 1945

Bernard Etxepare

¶Aduertant Impreſſor, & lectores quod.z.nunquam ponitur pro.m. Neq;.t. ante.i. pronunciatur pro.c. Et vbi virgula ponitur ſub.ç.hoc modo quod fit dum præ ponitur vocalibus.a.o.u.Tunc.c.pronunciabitur paulo aſperius quam.z.vt in.ce.ci.*

In this Basque edition, we have done our best to reproduce Etxepare's Basque as it was originally printed. There are many modern Basque renditions available, most notably the 1995 edition mentioned throughout this text. As this reproduces the original, we have retained some quirks such as the use of the "u" for the "v" and vice versa, used some characters that are no longer in common use, such as the "long s," ſ, the ligatures æ and ct, and letters no longer in use in Basque like ç and c. Therefore, for example, the word vſte is the modern Basque word uste or "opinion, view, or belief."

Regarding word breaks, we have endeavored to maintain the original, but have consulted modern Basque editions for occasionally where it is not clear if a word is broken or not. —eds.

A Note for Typesetter

Let the printer and readers be advised that z never goes in place of m nor should the t before i be pronounced as c and when c contains a cedilla which occurs when preceding a, o, and u, then c is pronounced as ce, ci, that is, harder than the z.

Erregueren aduocatu videzco eta nobleari irthute eta honguciez complituyari bere iaun eta iabe Bernard Leheteri bernard echeparecoac haren cerbitzari chipiac gogo honez goraynci baque eta oſſagarri Ceren baſcoac baitira abil animos eta gentil eta hetan içan baita eta baita ſciencia gucietan lettratu hahdiric miraz nago iauna nola batere ezten aſſayatu bere lengoage propriaren fauoretan heuſcaraz cerbait obra eguitera eta ſcributan imeitera ceren ladin publica mundu gucietara berce lengoagiac beçala hayn ſcribatzeco hondela. Eta cauſa honegatic gueldditzenda abataturic eceyn reputacione vague eta berce nacione oroc vſte dute ecin denſere ſcriba dayteyela lengoage hartan nola berce oroc baitute ſcribatzen beryan Eta ceren oray çuc iauna noble et naturazcoac beçala baytuçu eſtimatzen goratzen eta ohoratzen heuſcara çuri neure iaun eta iabia beçala igorten darauritzut heuſcarazco copblabatzu ene ignoranciaren araura eguinac. Ceren iauna hayec iqhuſſiric eta corregituric plazer duçun beçala irudi baçautzu imprimi eraci diçaçun eta çure eſcutic oroc dugum ioya ederra Imprimituric heuſcara orano içan eztena eta çure hatſe honetic dadin aitzinerat augmenta continua eta publica mundu gucietara eta baſcœc bercec beçala duten bere lengoagian ſcribuz cerbait doctrina eta plazer harceco ſolaz eguiteco cantatzeco eta denbora igaraiteco materia eta ginendirenec guero duten cauſa oboro haren abançatzeco eta obligatu guiren guciac geyncoari
Aij
othoyz eguitera dizum mundu honeten proſperoqui vicia eta bercian parabiçuya, Amen.

Dedication

To the righteous and noble King's counsel, who is most virtuous and kind, whom his Lord and Master Bernard Lehete, Bernard of Etxepare, his humble servant, cordially bids his respects, peace, and good health.

As the Basques are skilled, hard-working and genteel, with great men of letters having been and who are among them, I am amazed my Lord, how none, for the good of his own language, has attempted to undertake or write some work in Basque so that the whole world might know that it is as good as any tongue in which to write and this is the reason wherefore it is relegated, without any renown and why all the rest of the nations believe that nothing can be written in that tongue, even as all of the rest write in their own.

And as you, noble Lord of this land that you are, esteem, praise, and do honor to Basque, it is to you, my Lord and Master, to whom I am sending these verses wrought in my own ignorance; so that, my Lord, having seen and corrected them at your will, you might have them printed and that all of us might have, in this way, from your own hand, a precious jewel, the Basque language in print, something which has not existed hitherto; so that it might grow, endure, and spread throughout in the future from your auspicious beginning; and that the Basques might have in their language, in the same manner as the rest, some doctrine and written matter whereby they might amuse themselves, converse, sing, and spend their time, and in which upcoming generations might be motivated to perfect it; and that we might see it fit to pray unto God that He might grant you a prosperous life in this world and heaven in the next. Amen.

¶Doctrina Christiana.

1 Munduyãden guiçon oroc beharluque pẽſatu
Iangoycoac nola duyen batbedera formatu
Bere irudi propiara gure arima creatu
Memoriaz vorondatez endelguyaz goarnitu.

5 Eceyn iaunec eztu nahi muthilgaixtoa eduqui
Ez pagatu ſoldataric cerbiçatu gaberic
Iangoycua ariduçu hala hala gurequi
Gloriaric ez emanen hongui eguin gaberic

9 Muthilec gure cerbiçutan deramate vrthia
Soldata apphur bategatic harcen pena handia
Iangoycoac beharluque guc veçanbat valia
Cerbiçatu behardugu emaytecoz gloria.

13 Oguiric eztacuſſat vilcen haci ereyn gaberic
Norc cerhaci ereyn vilcendici comunqui
Obra honac vqhenendu goalardona frangoqui.
Bay etare beqhatuyac punicione ſegurqui.

17 Ceren ieyncoa egun oroz ongui ari bayçaygu
Guc ere hala behardugu harçaz vnſa orhitu
Gure hatſc eta fina hura dela penſatu
Goyz etarraz orhituqui haren icena laudatu.

Arraxian

21 Arraxian ecitian gomendadi ieyncoary
Eta othoy beguireçan perilgucietaric
Guero iraçar adinian orhit adi vertaric
Cenbaitere oracione erraytera deuotqui

1. The Christian Doctrine

1   Every man in this world should ponder
    how God has molded each and every one of us,
    how He has created our soul in His own image,
    and has endowed it with memory, understanding, and a free will.

5   No master desires to have a bad servant,
    nor to pay him without being served.
    God works in the same way with us.
    He will not give us glory if we do no good.

9   Servants go through the year serving us,
    and for a pittance put up with a thousand vexations.
    God should have His bit from us.
    We must serve Him to receive His glory.

13 I know not of wheat harvested without being sown,
    and generally each reaps what he sows.
    Fine works will have their ample reward,
    and sin is also sure to have its punishment.

17 Since God rewards us every day,
    we too should remember Him in gratitude,
    and ponder how He is our beginning and end,
    and how we should particularly praise His name night and day.

At Night

21 At night, when retiring, entrust thyself to God,
    and ask Him to protect thee from all evil.
    When thou awakest, remember then
    to recite thy prayers with devotion.

Goycian

25 Albadaguic ioanadi eliçara goycian
Ieyncoari han gomenda bere eche ſaynduyan
Han ſarcian penſa eçac aycinian norduyan
Norequila minço yçan han agoen artian.

Ilherrian

29 Hilez vnſa orhit adi ilherrian ſarçian
Hi nolaco ciradela viciciren artian
Hec veçala hil beharduc eta ez iaquin orduya
Othoy eguic ieyncoari deyen varcamenduya.

Batheyarria

33 Eliçara içanian ſoeguic bateyarrira
Penſa eçac handuyala recebitu fedia
Ieyncoaren gracia eta ſaluaçeco vidia
Hari eguin albaiteça lehen eçaguicia.

Gorpuz ſaynduya

37 Vertan guero ſo albaiteguinóden gorpuz ſainduya
Penſa eçac hura dela hire ſaluaçalia
Adoreçac deuocionez eta galde gracia
Azquen finian emandiaçan recebice dignia.

Curucea

41 Crucifica iqhus eta orhit adi orduyan
Nola yçan redemitu haren odol ſaynduyaz
Harc eryo haritudic hiri leyan vicia
Penſa ezac nola eman hari vere ordia.

Andredona Maria

45 Andere honaden leqhura ailchaiçac veguiac
Mundo oro eztaquidic hura veçayn valia
Ieyncoaren hurranena hura diagoc glorian
Graciac oro vere eſcuyan nahiduyen orduyan.

In the Morning

25   Go to church in the morning if thou canst;
      entrust thyself to God in His holy house,
      and when entering, ponder upon who stands before thee,
      and with whom thou speakest while there.

In the Churchyard

29   When entering the churchyard kindly remember the dead,
      think back that while they lived they were like thee
      Like them shalt thou die and thou knowest not when
      Ask God to grant them His forgiveness.

At the Baptismal Font

33   When going to church, look upon the baptistery,
      recall that it is there where thou didst receive thy faith,
      the grace of God, and the road to salvation;
      may thy first show of gratitude be for Him.

The Holy Sacrament

37   Then gaze upon where the Holy Sacrament lies,
      and ponder how He is thy saviour.
      Worship Him with devotion and ask Him for the grace
      of receiving Him worthily until the end of thy days.

The Cross

41   Gaze upon the crucifix and recall then
      how His holy blood was redeemed.
      He took death upon Himself to give thee life.
      Ponder upon how thou mightst pay Him in return.

Mother Mary

45   Look up to where the good Lady is found.
      Not even the whole world could help thee like her.
      She is the one closest to God in glory,
      and has at hand every grace she could want.

49　Oandere glorioſa eta ama eztia
　　çutan dago beqhatoren ſperança gucia
　　Ni çugana nyatorqueçu beqhatore handia
　　Arimaren ſaluacera çu çaquiztan valia.

Saynduyer

53　Saynduyer ere eguin eçac heure eçagucia
　　Singularqui nortan vaytuc heure deuocionia
　　Ceyn ſaynduren veſta daten orhit egun verian
　　Eta noren ycenetan fundatuden eliça
　　Orhituqui othoy eguin daquizquian valia

Oracione igandeco

58　Miſericordiaz bethe ciraden iaun eztia
　　Othoy ençun yaçadaçu neure oracionia
　　Biciniçan artian eta erioco phunduyan
　　çuc ydaçu othoy oſſo neure endelgamenduya
　　Alteratu gabetaric çure fede ſaynduyan
　　Gaucen vnſa eguiteco neure azquen finian.

64　Eta orduyan çuc ydaçu indar eta gratia
　　Beccatuyez vqheyteco vide dudan doluya
　　Perfectuqui eguiteco neure confeſſionia
　　Neure beqhatuyez oroz dudan varqhamenduya
　　Bay dignequi errecebi çure gorpuz ſaynduya
　　Bayetare vehardiren verce ſagramenduyac.

70　Exay gayça ginen vayta tentacera orduya
　　Nontic engana niroyen vere arte guciaz
　　Othoy iauna enguztaçu lagun cure ſaynduyac
　　Enexayac venci enaçan neure azquen finian.

74　Ene arima orduyan har othoy cure glorian
　　Nola vaita redemitu çure odol ſaynduyaz
　　Eta nic handacuſſadan çure veguitartia
　　Eta ſaynduyequi lauda çure mageſtatia

49   Oh, glorious Lady and sweet Mother!
      In Thee lies every hope of the sinner.
      I too, a great sinner, turn to Thee,
      for Thy help in the salvation of my soul.

The Saints

53   Show, as well, respect for the saints,
      especially the one of thy devotion.
      Remember whose feast day it is that day
      and to whom the church is dedicated.
      Ask them fervently to help thee.

Sunday Prayer

58   O kind, merciful Lord,
      hark, I pray, unto my prayer,
      in life and upon my deathbed.
      Grant me, I pray, all the faculties of my mind
      so that, without wavering in Thy holy faith,
      the affairs of my final hour might be in order.

64   And grant me then the strength and grace
      of duly repenting of my sins,
      and rightly making my confession
      in order to gain forgiveness for all my sins,
      to receive Thy holy body worthily,
      and the rest of the prescribed sacraments.

70   And since the devil will then come and tempt me,
      with all his cunning to find a way to deceive me,
      send Thy saints, o Lord, in my aid,
      lest the enemy should overcome me in my final hour.

74   Receive then, I pray, my soul in Thy glory,
      as it is with Thy holy blood that it has been redeemed
      that I might look upon Thy visage there,
      and honour Thy majesty in communion with the saints.

78 Goyz etarraſtz eguitenduc buluz eta vezticia
Gorpuçaren cerbiçutan barazcari afaria
Arimaren ſaluaçeco ieyncoaren ohorian
Eçayala othoy neque gauça hoyen eguitia
Egun oroz ecin vada aſte oroz igandian

83 Gure artian haur dacusſat ixutarçum handia
Nola dugun cerbiçacen hanbat gure exaya
Iangoycua deſconoci gure ſaluaçalia
Eta oroc eçagucen dela videgabia

87 Anhiz gendez miraz nago neureburuyaz lehenic
Nola gauden múdu hunequi hayn vorthizqui ioſſiric
Hanbat gende dacuſcula hunec enganaturic
Oranocoac ygorritu oro buluzcorriric
Eta eztute guerocoec hantic eſcapaceric

92 Perſonoro hildenian hirur çathi eguiten
Gorpuzori vſtelcera lur hoçian egoyzten
Vnharçuna ahaidiec vertan dute particen
Arima gaixoa dabilela norat ahaldaguien
Hayn viage vortician compaynia faltacen

97 Orhituqui ygandian vehardugu penſatu
Cenbatetan eguin dugun aſte hartan beccatu
Orhit eta ieyncoari barqhamendu eſcatu
Atorra nola arimere aſte oroz garbitu.

101 Bi pundutan diagoçu gure gauça gucia
Hongui eguin vadaçagu ſegur parabiçuya
Beqhatutan hil dadina bertan comdenatuya
Berce videric ecin date hobenari beguira.

105 Ehonere eztacuſat hayn laxoden arçaynic
Oxoa hencen eztuyenic bere ardietaric
Gure arimaz cargo dugu iangoycuac emanic
Nola gobernacendugun batbederac ſobegui
Condu herſi vehardugu harçaz eman ſegurqui
Nori baitu vereodolaz carioqui eroſſi
Hala cinex eztaçana dauque enganaturic.

78 Thou dost dress and undress in the morning and at night,
thou dost eat and sup on behalf of thy body.
Thus, to save thy soul for the glory of God,
be not repelled from doing those acts;
if unable every day, then every week on Sundays.

83 This is the great blindness I see in ourselves
in which we work to please our enemy so,
and ignore God, our Saviour,
even in our recognition of this injustice.

87 I am astounded to see how many of us, I the first among them,
are so strongly tied to this world,
in spite of seeing so many deceived by him.
Those living until now he cast out naked,
and those in the future may not get away.

92 When every one dies there are three phases:
the body is buried under the cold earth to rot;
his possessions are shared out among his debtors;
the poor soul travels on to where it may,
lacking company on such an uneasy journey.

97 On Sundays thou shouldst carefully ponder
how many times thou hast sinned that week.
Ponder and then ask God for His forgiveness;
cleanse thy soul every week as thou wouldst a shirt.

101 Our fate hangs upon two matters:
If thou hast done good works, paradise is assured.
He who dies in sin, is then damned.
There's no other way, look to the one who's best.

105 I know not where there is a shepherd so derelict
that he fails to chase a wolf away from his flock.
We are entrusted by God to the care of our souls.
Just look at the stewardship of each one of us.
We are sure to be held strictly accountable
to the one who redeemed it with His blood at such a high price.
He who believes this not is deceived.

112 Contemplatu vehardugu paſſione ſaynduya
Eta ſendi vihocian haren pena handia
Nola çagoen curucian oro çauriz bethia
Huyn eſcuyac içaturic eta vuluzcorria

116 Ohoynequi vrcaturic nola gayzquiguilia
Eta arhancez coroaturic mundu ororen iabia
Haren gorpuz precioſo eta delicatuya
Gayzqui eſcarniaturic eta çathicatuya.

120 Elas orduyan nola çagoen haren arima triſtia
Haren ama maytia eta mundu ororen habia
Pena hetan ecuſteaz bere ſeme maytia
Eta hilcen veguietan mundu ororen vicia.

124 Viocian dirauſtaçu guertuz ama eztia
çure orduco doloriac eta vihoz çauriac
Beguiez nola cenacuſan çure iabe handia
Orotaric laryola odol preciatuya
Hec nigatic ciradela arinuçu qhonduya.

129 Orhit adi nola duyan eguin anhiz beqhatu
Heyen cauſaz merexitu anhicetan hondatu
Bere miſericordiaz nola huyen guardatu
Eta dolu vqhen vaduc vertan oro barqhatu
Eta aguian hic eguinen vertan verriz beqhatu.

134 Orhit adi iengoycoaren mageſtate handiaz
Ceruya lurra ychaſoa daduçala eſcuyan
Saluacia damnacia eryoa eta vicia
Eſtendicen orotara haren poteſtatia
Eci eſcapa hari ehor dauguinian manuya.

139 Mundu honetan vadirogu batac bercia engana
Bana vercian eguiatic batbedera ioanenda
Nor nolaco içan guiren orduyan aguerico da
Eguin erran penſatuyac aguerico guciac.

143 Orhit adi ieyncoaren inſticia handiaz
Nola oroc vehardugun eman qhondu herſia
Eguin oroz recebitu gure merexituya
Eryoa dauguinian vayta haren meçuya.

112 We must contemplate the Sacred Passion
and feel the great sorrow in his heart;
how He was upon the cross, riddled with wounds,
with His hands and feet nailed fast and His body naked.

116 Put to death with thieves like a criminal,
crowned in thorns, the Lord of the world,
His precious, delicate body
vilely mocked and shattered.

120 Alas, how must his anguished Mother have felt,
his beloved mother and the mainstay of the whole world,
when she saw her beloved Son in such agony,
dying before her eyes, the life of all the world!

124 My heart truly bleeds for Thee, o sweet Mother.
That sorrow and those wounds in Thy heart on that day,
to see Thy beloved master in such a way with Thine eyes
while His precious blood flowed out;
I know very well that it was for me.

129 Remember that thou hast committed many a sin,
for which thou hast often deserved damnation.
Thou hast been spared on account of His compassion,
and if thou hast repented, He has at once forgiven thee.
And still dost thou return to thy sinning ways!

134 Remember the immense majesty of God.
The earth, the sky, and the sea are in His hands
as are salvation, damnation, life and death.
His power extends overall.
No one may flee from Him when He commands.

139 In this world, yea, we may fool each other
but in the other world everyone will walk in truth.
There will it be out what each has done.
All will be revealed: acts, utterances, thoughts.

143 Remember the grand justice of God,
how we are all to face the reckoning,
and receive our just reward for our acts;
when Death, His messenger, comes.

147 Ordu hartan afer date hari apellacia
    Harc ehori eztemayo oren vaten epphia
    Ecetare eſtimacen chipia ez handia
    Batvederac egarrico orduyan vere haxia.

151 Orduyan cer eguinendut gaixo beqhataria
    Arartecoac faltaturen contra iuge handia
    Abocacen eztaquique ehorc haren gortian
    Oguen oro publicoqui aguerturen orduyan.

155 Elas othoy oroc eguin oray penitencia
    Behar orduyan eztuquegu guero aguian aizina
    Anhiz iende enganatu doa luçamenduyaz
    Seguraturic ehorc eztu egun vaten vicia.

159 Guguirade egun oroz heryoaren azpian
    Behardugu preſt eduqui gure gauça gucia
    Gure gaucez ordenatu oſſo guiren artian
    Guero eztugun eguiteco heçaz azquen finian
    Arimaz aſquieguiteco vaduquegu orduyan.

164 Penſa othoy nola gauden bi bideren erdian
    Salva bano damnaçeco perileco punduyan
    Ehor fida eztadila othoy vanitatian
    Saynduyac eçiraden ſarthu vanitatez glorian.

168 Elas othoy hunat veha beqharore gucia
    Beqhatuyaz damnacendu iangoycuac munduya
    Ceren hanbat veccatutan deramagu vicia
    Eta guhaurc gure faltaz galcen gureburuya.

172 Arzayn oroc vilcenditu ardiac arraxaldian
    Leqhu honerat eramayten eguraldi gaycian
    Batbederac penſa veça arimaren gaynian
    Nola ſaluaturen duen hura vere finian.

176 Beqhatorec yfernuyan dute pena handia
    Pena handi ycigarri eceyn pauſu gabia
    Seculacoz egon vehar hango ſugar vician
    çuhur denac hara eztohen eguin penitencia.

147 Then shall it be in vain to appeal to Him,
no one shall be granted the space of an hour,
nor shall there be a distinction made between rich and poor.
There each shall bear his burden.

151 What is to become of me, a poor sinner?
Mediators shall be wanting, with the great Judge as my adversary.
No one shall be able to act as a lawyer at the Judgment.
There shall all transgressions be made public.

155 Alas, I pray, let us all do penitence!
For we may not be able to in the hour of need;
many people fool themselves by forestalling,
yet no one is assured even a single day of life.

159 Every day we are faced with Death;
all out affairs must be in order,
take care of them while in good health.
Let us not deal with them when the end comes,
for we shall have enough upon our hands with our souls!

164 Let us be aware that we are at a crossroads
leading more toward damnation than salvation.
May no one trust, I pray, his vanity;
for no saint ever entered heaven through vanity.

168 Alas, may every sinner take heed of this, I pray!
God condemns the world for its sin.
Wherefore, then, comes so much sinful living
when it is we ourselves who are to blame for our perdition?

172 Every shepherd gathers his flock at nightfall;
he leads them to shelter in bad weather;
may each reflect upon his soul,
upon how to save it in the final hour.

176 Great is the torment of the sinners in hell;
an enormous, horrifying, never ending torment.
In that great inferno are they to remain for all eternity
May the wise do penitence that they might not end there.

Harmac eryoaren contra

180 Eryoa iauguitenda gutivſte denian
Eta aguian ez emanen confeſſione epphia
Hirur gauça albaditu ehorc ere eguiaz
Nola ere hil vaytadi doha ſalumenduyan.

Lehen eguia

184 O iaun hona aytor cendut beqhatore niçala
Eta gaizqui eguitiaz oguen handi dudala
Nic vaycitut offenſatu bide eztudan veçala
Dolu dicit eta damu çure contra eguinaz.

Bigareen eguia

188 Oiaun hona gogo dicit oren preſent honetan
Goardaceco beqhaturic viciniçan artian
Othoy iauna çuc ydaçu indar eta gracia
Gogo honetan yrauteco neure vici gucian.

Heren eguia

192 Oiaun hona gogo dicit gariçuma denian
Eguiazqui eguiteco neure confeſſionia
Vayetare compliceco didan penitencia
Othoy iauna çuc confirma ene vorondatia.

196 Eta hoyec eguiazquiehorc hala ezpaditu
Albayliaqui duda gabe ecin dateyela ſalbu
Bere beqhatuyac oro vaditu ere confeſſatu
Eta hala çinhex beça nahi eztenac enganatu.

200 Apezeq ez apezpicuq ezetare aytafaynduc
Abſoluacen halacoaren eceyn bothereric eztu
Iangoycua bethiere vihocera ſodiagoçu
Guhaurc vano ſegurago gure gogua diacuxu
Gogua gabe hura vaytan hiçac oro afertuçu.

Weapons against Death

180 Death intrudes when least expected.
      And, perhaps, leaves no time for confession.
      He that truly practices these three things
      shall be saved, no matter how he dies.

First Truth

184 O Good Lord, I confess I am a sinner,
      and am guilty of doing bad.
      Now that I have unduly offended thee,
      it weighs heavily upon me and I repent having sinned against Thee.

Second Truth

188 O Good lord! I hereby promise
      to refrain from sin all my days.
      Lord, please give me strength and grace
      to persevere with this resolution all my days.

Third Truth

192 O Good Lord! I promise that for Lent
      I shall make a proper confession,
      and fulfill the penitence put by my confessor.
      Lord, strengthen my will!

196 If anyone will not fulfill these things,
      let him know there is surely no salvation for him,
      even if he has confessed of all his sins;
      let whoever would not be fooled believe.

200 Neither priest nor bishop nor even pope
      are able to absolve such a one.
      God always looks into the heart.
      He knows our mind better than ourselves,
      for without our mind, are all our words hollow before Him.

205   Regla eçac egun oroz onſa heure etchia
Eure gauça gucietan emac diligencia
Eta eure trabayluya duyan penitencia
Iangoycua lauda eçac gauça ororen buruyan.

209   Honequila albayteça bethiere conuerſa
Gaixtœqui ecin ayte gayzqui beci prouecha
Bercer eguin eztaçala nahi eçuqueyena
Ezetare falta ere hiaurc nahi duyana
Legue honi ſegui vedi ſalbu nahiduyena.

Hamar manamenduyac:

214   Adoreçac iágoycobat onheſtz oroz gaynetic
Haren ycena ez iura cauſa gabe vanoqui
Ygandiac eta veſtac ſanctifica deuotqui
Ayta eta ama ohoraiçac vici yçan lucequi
Ehor erho eztaçala ezetare gaycetſi
Norc veria vayecila emazteric ez hunqui
Vercerena eztaçala ebaxi ez eduqui
Fama gayciq eztemala lagunari falſuqui
Bercen emazte alabac ez deſira gayxtoqui
Eçetare vnhaſuna lecotbedi iuſtoqui.

224   Manamenduyac hoyec dira iangoycuac emanic
Hoc veguira diçagula ſalua guiten hegatic.

Indicio generala

226   Iudicio generalaz nola orhit eztira
Beccatutan vici dira bethi vere ayſira
Egun hartan gal ezquiten aycinetic veguira
Han orduyan eztuquegu ehorc ere ayzina
Harçan vnſa orhitcia çuhurcia handida.

231   Arma arma mundu oro iudicio handira
Ceru eta lur ororen creadore handia
Munduyaren iuyacera rigoroſqui helduda
Nola gauden apphaynduric batbederac beguira.

205   Tidy thy house well with every day.
      Be diligent in all thou dost.
      And may penitence be thy work.
      Praise God after finishing each chore.

209   Always deal with the good,
      for with the bad canst thou only beget ill.
      Do not to others which thou wouldst not want for thyself.
      Do not fail to do what thou wouldst want for thyself;
      may he who wishes salvation follow this law.

The Ten Commandments

214   Worship but one God, love Him above all else;
      Thou shalt not take His name in vain;
      Thou shalt keep the feast days and Sabbath holy;
      Thou shalt honor thy father and thy mother to live a long life;
      Thou shalt not kill nor hate anyone;
      Thou shalt not steal nor possess other than thine own;
      Thou shalt not bear false witness;
      Thou shalt not desire the wife or daughter of another;
      Nor their possessions unless warranted.

224   These are the commandments given by God.
      Let us observe them to be saved by them.

The Universal Judgment

226   As they do not ponder the universal judgment,
      they live ever blissfully in sin.
      Let us be forewarned lest we should be lost on that day,
      for then shall none of us have time.
      'Tis wisest to reflect upon it well.

231   Hark, hark, all are to be judged!
      The Supreme Creator of heaven and earth
      is come to judge the world harshly.
      How is each one of us prepared?

235 Manamendu ygortendu mundugucietaric
Gende oro bat daquion ioſafaten vilduric
Ehon ere ehor ere eſcapatu gaberic.
Ceru eta lur gucia daude yqharaturic.

239 Eryoa manacendu eceyn falta gaberic
Hilac oro dacacela aycinera viciric
Hantic harat eztuquela vothereric iagoytic
Mundu oro iarrirenda bi lecutan herſiric
Glorian ezpa yfernuyan ezta eſcapaceric.

244 Manacendu yfernuya andi eta vortizqui
Handirenac ygoriçan luçamendu gaberic
Arima eta gorpucetan nahi tuyela icuſſi
Eta emanen darayela cer vaytute mereci.

248 Gende honac onſa penſa iuge hunen gaynian
Nola duyen gucietan poteſtate handia
Eryoan yfernuyan ceru eta lurrian
Ceren dabil haren contra vada veqhatoria.

252 Gure artian haur dacuſſat ixutarçun handia
Nola dugun cerbiçacen hanbat gure exaya
Iangoycoa deſconoci gure ſaluaçalia
Eta oroc eçaguçen dela vide gabia.

256 Harren bier emanendu ſentencia piçuya
Elgarre qui pena diten ifernuco garrian
Seculaco ſuyan eta eceyn pauſu gabian
Oroc othoy onſa penſa cerden yrabacia.

260 Egundano ezta içan ez içanen iagoytic
Iudicio hayn handiric ezetare vorthizich
Sortu eta ſorcecoac hilez guero pizturic
Oroc hara vehar dute eſcuſatu gaberic.

264 Anhiz gauça vehardira iudicio handian
Iugeac duyen poteſtate parte ororen gaynian
Demandantac erran deçan vere cauſa eguiaz
Bayetare defendentac bere defenſionia
Porogatu datenian norc duqueyen çucena
Sentenciaz eman deçan iugiac nori veria.

235 He gives the order that from every world,
  all should go and gather before Him in Joshaphat;
  that no one anywhere may escape;
  all in Heaven and on Earth are trembling.

239 He commands Death to bring before Him
  all of the dead brought back to life without fail.
  Henceforth shall it have no sway;
  everyone shall be kept in two places:
  If not in glory then in perdition; there is no deliverance.

244 He orders hell solemnly and sternly
  to send forthwith those dwelling within.
  He wishes to see them in body and in soul,
  and He will mete out their just reward.

248 Good people, think well of this Judge
  about how he wields great power throughout,
  over death, hell, heaven, and earth.
  Why, then, does the sinner go against Him?

252 This is the great blindness I see in ourselves
  in which we work to please our enemy so,
  and ignore God, our Saviour,
  even in our recognition of this injustice.

256 He will pass a stern sentence on both [body and soul],
  so that both will suffer in the flames of hell,
  in that eternal, ever-burning fire.
  All of ye think, I pray, wherein lies your gain?

260 Hitherto has there never been nor ever will there be
  such a solemn and strict judgment.
  Those born and who are yet to be born, resurrected after death,
  all are to be there, none excused.

264 Many a thing is required in a great judgment:
  The Judge must have jurisdiction over all parties,
  the prosecutor is to state his case truthfully;
  likewise the defendant with his defense.
  When it be proven who is right,
  the Judge is to pass sentence, each one receiving his due.

270 Egun hartan iuge date mundu ororen iabia
Baytu ororen gaynian poteſtate handia
Acuſari vera date eta conciencia
Beqhatu oro publicoqui aguerico orduyan

274 Beqhatoren contra date orduyan mundu gucia
Cerenduten ofenditu hayen creaçalia
Ordu hartan ixildauque triſte veqhatoria
Orotaric cerraturic daude pauſſu guciac.

278 Iuge iauna iraturic egonenda gaynetic
Yreſtera apphaynduric yfernuya azpitic
Exay gayça acuſacen ezquerreco aldetic
Beccatuyac eſcuynetic minçaturen publiqui
Hire contra heben guituc ihaurorrec eguinic
Gayzquienic contra date conciença varnetic.

284 Eſtalceco ez içanen ehon ere leqhuric
Aguercera norc eguinen ordu hartan vathiric
Mundu oro egonenda hayen contra Iarriric
Saynduac ere ordu hartan oro egonen ixilic
Iugeac ere ez ençunen ezeyn ere othoyc
Egun harçaz orhit guiten othoy hara gaberic.

290 Nondirate egun hartan hebengo iaun erreguiac
Duque conde marques çaldun eta verce iaun nobliac
Eta hayen armadaco guiçon ſendoen valentiac
ordu hartan valiaco guti hayen potenciac.

294 Iuriſta eta theologo pœta eta doctoriac
Procurador aduocatu iuge eta notariac
Ordu hartan aguerico clarqui hayen maliciac
Eta guti valiaco cautela eta parleriac..

298 Ayta ſayndu cardenale apphez eta prelatuyac
Berez eta ardi oroz eman vehar han conduya
Egun hartan handiena yçanenda erratuya
Eta vardin iuyaturen handia eta chipia.

270 On that day shall the Judge be the master of the world
    as He has great power over all;
    He shall be the accuser as well as the conscience;
    then shall all sins be made known.

274 All the world shall be against the sinner
    for having offended their Creator.
    The miserable sinner shall be struck dumb.
    All around is every way out closed to him.

278 The Lord Judge shall be indignant from on high.
    From below shall hell be ready to swallow him up.
    On his left shall the wicked devil be accusing,
    on his right shall his sins be proclaiming:
    "Here we are, acting against thee, created by thee."
    The gravest shall be from within the conscience itself.

284 There will be no place at all to hide.
    Who would dare come forward at such a time?
    Everyone shall be set against him,
    even all the saints shall remain silent at that point;
    Nor shall the Judge hear any plea.
    Let us bear this in mind before going there.

290 Where will this world's lordly kings be?
    The dukes, earls, marquesses, and other nobles,
    and the feats of the mighty men in their army?
    At that time shall their might be of little use.

294 Jurists and theologians, poets and doctors,
    attorneys, lawyers, judges, and notaries.
    Then shall their ignoble acts be revealed,
    And their judiciousness and prattle will be of little use.

298 Popes, cardinals, priests, and prelates,
    will have to bear full account of themselves and their flock.
    On that day shall the greatest be damned,
    and the great and small shall be judged alike.

302 Aferdate egun hartan hari apellacia
Ehon ere eztaçagu iaunic vere gaynian
Malicia gayci çayca eta mayte eguia
Elas othoy oroc eguin oray penitencia
Egun hartan guero eztugun eguiteco handia.

307 Seynaliac ginendira aicinetic trifteric
Elementac ebiliren oro tribulaturic
Iguzquia ilhargui odoletan ecinic
Ychafoa famurturic goyti eta veheyti
Hango arraynac icituric ebiliren ialguiric.

312 Eta lurra icigarri oro iqharaturic
çuhamuyec dacartela odolezco ycerdi
Tenpeftatez igorciriz ayre oro famurric
Mendi eta harri oro elgar çaticaturic
Mundu oro iarrirenda fuyac arrafaturic.

317 Iuge iaunac manaturen vera iauguin gaberic
Gauça oro xahu deçan vehin fuyac lehenic
Saxu eta quirax oro dohen mundu gucitic
Eta hal iarrirenda lurgucia erreric.

321 Trompetada minçaturen mundugucietaric
Hilac oro iayqui huna çuyen hobietaric
Arima eta gorpucetan oro vertan pizturic
Oroc hara vehar dugu efcufatu gaberic.

325 Iuftu oro yganenda hertan goyti ayrian
Eta egonen efcoynetic iugearen aldean
Beccatoreac dolorezqui fugarrian lurrian
Hariqu eta dançuteno fentencia gaynian.

329 Dagœnian gende oro aicinian vilduric
Iauguinenda rigorofqui faynduyequi cerutic
Iofaften egonenda airian gora iarriric
Beccatorer eguinendu arrangura handiric
Haren hiçac eçarriren oro erdiraturic.

302 It will be useless to appeal against Him.
     For He recognizes no lord above Him.
     He abhors evil and loves truth.
     Alas, I pray, let us all do penitence
     to avoid such a great plight on that day.

307 Warnings shall sound mournfully beforehand;
     the elements shall be in upheaval,
     the sun and moon turned to blood,
     the sea heaving up and down.
     The fish therein shall jump out of fear.

312 And the earth shall quake terribly.
     Trees shall sweat a bloody sap.
     The air shall be racked by storms and thundering;
     with all the mountains and rocks crumbling against each other,
     and all the earth razed by fire.

317 The Lord Judge, before his appearance, shall order
     fire to cleanse all things at the outset.
     Let all filth and stench vanish from the whole world,
     and thus shall the whole earth be scorched.

321 A trumpet shall sound throughout the world:
     "Arise all ye dead and come hither from your tombs
     now that your bodies and souls are resurrected!"
     All of us are to go thither, unexcused.

325 The just shall rise up through the air,
     and shall sit to the right of the Judge.
     The sinners shall writhe upon the burning earth
     until they hear their sentence passed.

329 And when all are gathered before Him,
     he shall swoop down from the heavens with the saints.
     He will sit in Joshaphat on high.
     He shall chide the sinners.
     His words will leave them all distraught.

334 Hartu nahiçuyenian paffione fayndua
     Haren contra gincenian armaturic gendia
     Hiz huxbatez icituric egocitu lurrian
     Iuyacera dauguinian mageftate handian
     Nola eztu loxaturen ordu hartan munduya.

339 Erranendu beccatorer dolorezqui orduyan
     Niçaz ecineten orhit bicicinetenian
     Hanbat ongui nic eguinic çuyer çuyen mendian
     Efquer honbat vqhen eztut çuyeganic vician.

343 Cerere hon vaytuçuye oro dira eniac
     Gorpuz eta hon guciac baietare arimac
     çuyendaco eguin ditut lurra eta çeruyac
     Yguzquia ilharguia eta fructu guciac.

347 Suyac vero hurac xahu hax harceco ayria
     Aynguruyac çuyen goarda ararteco faynduyac
     çuyegatic eçarridut guero neure vicia
     Hoyegatic orogatic cerda çuyen paguya.

351 Icuffiric anhicetan beharrian pobria
     Eri goffe egarria eta buluzcorria
     Ene ycenian anhicetan galdeguinic limofna
     çuyec vqhen baytuçuye heçaz guti anfia.

355 Bay erhoqni conplacitu ene contra exaya
     Demonio haraguia bayetare munduya
     Oray dela çuyendaco maradicionia
     Ifernuco fuya eta iagoytico nequia
     Eta çuyen conpaynia demonio gucia.

360 Ezta anhiz luçaturen execucionia
     Bertan date yrequiren lurra oren verian
     Su harequi irexiren oro vere varnian
     Haur yçanen veccatoren vndar yrabacia.

364 Elas nola yçanenden heben damu handia
     Damu handi içigarri remedio gabia
     Hanbat iende feculacoz damnaturen denian
     O iaun huna çuc guiçaçu othoy hantic veguira.

334 When He wished to go through with the Holy Passion,
people came out against Him in arms.
With a single word He caused them to cower in fear.
In coming to judge so majestically,
how could He fail to humble the world?

339 Then shall He say to sinners in a sad voice:
"Ye forgot me while ye lived.
In spite of the good I did for you throughout your lives,
I received not the slightest bit of your gratitude."

343 "Whatever good ye have is from me:
your bodies and all your belongings as well as your souls.
For you I made heaven and earth,
the sun, the moon, and all fruits."

347 "Fire which warms, water which cleans, air to breathe,
your guardian angels, intercessors.
Thereafter I gave my life for you;
In recompense what did ye give in return?"

351 "When seeing the pauper in need time after time,
in sickness, in hunger, athirst, and naked,
and when asked for alms in my name,
ye worried not in the least for him."

355 "Ye did please the devil by going against me eagerly.
By going the way of the demon, the flesh, and the world.
Now is the time for your curse,
hellfire and eternal damnation,
and ye may have all of the demons as companions."

360 The execution thereof shall not wait for long.
Forthwith shall the earth open up.
All shall be engulfed in that fire.
This shall be the last wages of the sinner.

364 Alas, then, how great shall their sorrow be,
an immense, terrible, and unredeemable sorrow
when so many are to be damned for all eternity!
Good Lord, protect us, I pray, from such a plight.

368 Veretara içuliren ditu guero veguiac
Goacen oro elgarrequi ene adiſquidiac
Bethi eta ſeculacoz gauden ene glorian
Deſir oro conplituric alegria handian.

372 Hantic harat ezta içanen bi erretatu bayeci
Damnatuyac ifernuyan bethi dolorerequi
Saluatuyac ieyncoarequi bethi alegueraqui
Iangoycuac daguiela gure partia hoyequi.

376 Ceruya ezta ebiliren hantic harat iagoytic
Yguzquia egonenda orienten gueldiric
Ilharguia occidenten beguiz begui iarriric
Egun honec yraunendu eben eta iagoytic
Albana ez içanen heben gauça viciric.

381 O iaun hona çucirade gure creaçalia
Beccatore baguirere oro guira çuriac
Gure faltaz gal eztadin othoy çure eguina
Beccaturic garbizaçu othoy gure arimac.

385 Baldin eridevten vada gutan falta handia
Are duçu handiago çutan pietatia
çuretaric guiren othoy eguiguçu gracia
çure ama anderia daquigula valia.

Oracionia

389 Ave maria anderia gracia oroz bethia
Ieyncoaren ama virgin verac ordenatuya
Ceru eta lur ororen erreguina dignia
Beqhatoren aduocata eta confortaria.

393 Ni çugana niatorqueçu beccatore handia
Carioqui othoycera çuçaquiztan valia
Digne ezpaniz aypacera çure ycen ſaynduya
Ez gitera aycinera ceren bayniz ſaxuya.

368 He will then turn his eyes to his flock:
"Let us all go together, my friends
to be in my glory for ever and ever,
joyfully, where all desires shall be satisfied to the fullest."

372 Thenceforth shall there be but two kingdoms:
One for the damned, forever anguishing in hell;
one for the saved, forever rejoicing with God.
May God allow us to be with the latter.

376 Heaven shall thenceforth no longer tremble,
the sun shall be fixed in the east,
with the moon set just opposite in the west.
Thenceforth, shall that day last forever and ever,
but here shall there be no living thing.

381 O Good Lord, Thou art our Creator,
sinners though we are, we are all Thine.
Let not Thy creation be lost through our fault.
Cleanse our souls, we pray, of our sins.

385 Should there be any great fault within us,
greater still is the piety within Thee.
Grant us, we pray, the grace of being Thine;
may Thy Holy Mother protect us!

Prayer

389 Hail, Mary, our Lady full of grace,
called to be the Mother Virgin of God Himself;
Great Queen of all heaven and earth,
advocate and comforter to sinners.

393 I, come unto thee, a great sinner,
to ask earnestly of Thee to help me.
Unworthy though I am to speak Thy holy name,
nor to be in Thy presence, unclean that I am.

397 Miſericordiaz bethe ciren andere handia
Enaçaçula othoy yrayz eta ez menoſprecia
çuc guibela badidaçu elas ama eztia
Ordu hartan diacuſaçut galdu neure buruya.

401 Hanbat nuçu gauça orotan ni verthute gabia
Oren oroz beccatutan nabilena galduya
Eta bethi erratyua nola ardi yxuya
Mundu hunec haraguiac bethi enganatuya.

405 çu baicira gracia ororen ama eta yturburuya
Verthute eta hon gucien theſorera handia
Egundano beccatutan maculate gabia
Verthutetan ſeguiçeco eguidaçu gracia.

409 çutan dago beccatoren remedio gucia
Sperança oſſagarri eta ſaluamenduya
çuc guibela demaçuna nola vayta galduya
çure gomenduyan dena halaverda ſalbuya.

413 Ieyncoac çuri emandici poteſtate handia
Haren ama ciren guero ama ere maytia
Ceru eta lur orotan duçun hanbat valia
Cer çuc galde baytaguiçu den conplitugucia.

417 Eta çure eſcutic duten verce oroc gracia
Eta ſalua çuc deçaçun çuri gomendatuya
O andere excelente eceyn pare gabia
Saluatuyetaric niçan eguidaçu gracia.

421 çuri gomendacen nuçu hila eta vicia
Neure gorpuz eta arima eta dudan gucia
Othoy vehar orduyetan çuçaquiçat valia
Eta othoy çuc goberna ene vici gucia.

425 Eta yrabaz ieyncoaganic indar eta gracia
Beccatuyez eguiteco vnſa penitencia
Eta guero verthutetan deramadan vicia
Eta eguin gauça orotan haren vorondatia.

397　Great Lady, who is most merciful,
　　do not, I pray, reject nor despise me,
　　for alas, my sweet Mother, if Thou dost turn away from me,
　　my doom is therein sealed.

401　I am so lacking in virtue in everything,
　　being one who is ever sinning,
　　and always straying like a blind sheep,
　　always deceived by the flesh and this world.

405　As Thou art the Mother and source of all grace,
　　a great treasurer of all virtue and good,
　　never tainted by sin,
　　grant me the grace to carry on virtuously.

409　Within Thee lies all relief for sinners,
　　Hope, health, and salvation;
　　Doomed is he who turns his back upon Thee,
　　whereas he who enjoys Thy protection is saved.

413　God has granted Thee great power,
　　as Thou art His mother, indeed a beloved mother,
　　for Thou hast such favor throughout heaven and earth,
　　that whatever Thou mightst ask is granted,

417　that through Thee all the others might gain grace,
　　and that he who entrusts himself unto Thee may be saved by Thee.
　　O fine and incomparable Lady,
　　grant me the grace to be among those saved.

421　I entrust myself unto Thee in life and death,
　　my body, my soul and all I own.
　　Help me, I pray, in my hour of need
　　and, I pray, rule over all my life,

425　and attain from God the strength and grace
　　to do proper penitence for my sins,
　　to live henceforth a righteous life,
　　and to do His will in all things.

429 Beguira orthoy meſcabutic ene gorpuz pobria
Beccatutan hil eznadin eguidaçu gracia
Seculacos damnaturic enoyan galduya
Bana çure eſcutic dudan ſaluaceco vidia.

433 Eta guero dauguinian ene eryocia
Arimaren particeco oren ycigarria
Ordu hartan behar baytut eman condu herſia
Eguin oroz recebitu neure merexituya.

437 Eta ez iaquin lehen gaoyan nondaten oſtatuya
Ezetare çu ezpacira nordaquidan valia
Ordu hartan helçaquiçat othoy ama eztia
Ararteco leyal eta neure ayutaria.

441 Othoy çure gomenduyan har arima triſtia
Ordu hartan io ezteçan yfernuco vidia
çure ſeme iaunarequi eguidaçu baquia
Beccatuyac barqhaturic didan parabiçuya.

445 Eta nic handacuſadan çure veguitartia
Eta ſaynduyequi lauda haren mageſtatia
çeren vnſa orhit citen niçaz ama eztia
Gogo honez erranendut çuri ave maria.
Oracione haur derrana andredona maria
Othoy gomendatu duçun hila eta vicia.

429 Protect my poor body, I pray, from all misfortune.
     Grant me the grace not to die in sin,
     and not to be damned for eternity,
     but rather led by Thee down the road to salvation,

433 and then, when my death comes,
     the dreadful hour when the soul departs,
     the hour in which I shall be held strictly accountable,
     and receive the just reward for my deeds.

437 And not knowing at which inn I shall stay the first night,
     And not having anyone, if not Thou, to protect me;
     help me then, I pray, sweet Mother,
     faithful intercessory and abettor of mine.

441 Take, I pray, my sorrowful soul under Thy wing
     so that at that hour it will not head for damnation.
     Reconcile me with the Lord Thy Son,
     so that my sins are forgiven and paradise given.

445 May I see Thy countenance,
     and praise be to His Majesty in the communion of saints.
     For Thou dost remember me well, sweet Mother,
     I shall cheerfully say unto thee: Hail Mary.
     Whoever says this prayer, my lady St. Mary,
     consider him, I pray, as having entrusted himself in life and death.

¶Amoroſen gaztiguya

1 Bercec berceric gogoan eta nic andredona maria
  Andre hona daquigula gucior othoy valia.

3 Amoroſac nahi nuque honat veha valite
  Honliçaten gaztiguric aguian enzun liroyte
  Amore bat hautaceco conſey lubat nequeye
  Balinetan ſeculacoz gogoan ſar valequie.

7 Ni haurc ere vqhen dicit ceynbaytere amore
  Bana hantic eztut vqhen prouechuric batere
  Anhiz pena arima gal hanera eta neuryere
  Amoretan plazer baten mila dira dolore.

11 Amoretan othedate leyal denic batere
   Hiz ederrez ezpa ioyaz mutha eztadin hura ere
   Hoben vſta duyenori anhicetan traydore
   Hobena date gayzenic arimaren berere

15 Beqhatuzco amoria bethi date traydore
   Erioa dauguinian eguia çogueridate
   Hartuduten plazer oro orduyan yragandate
   Beccatuya gueldicenda penaçeco guero ere
   Anhiz plazer vqhen badu anhiz vehardolore.

20 Amorebat nahi nuque liadutanic eguia
   Vici eta hilez guero hayn laquidan valia
   Cerbiçatu nahi nuque halacoa vician
   Heben labur viciada iagoyticoz bercia.

24 Mundu oro iraganic ez eriden berceric
   Ieyncoaren ama hona gracia oroz betheric
   Haren amore içateco ezta ehor digneric
   Vnſa cerbiça daçagun mayte guitu bertaric.

2. Disappointment between Lovers

1   Others may have someone else in their thoughts but for me 'tis St. Mary;
this good Lady who helps us all.

3   I should like lovers to pay attention
for they will surely hear valuable counsel.
I should give them counsel on how to find true love.
May it be etched forever in their minds.

7   I, too, have had some loves,
but from them I benefited not at all;
only great grief, a lost soul, both hers and mine;
for one pleasure in love there are a thousand sorrows.

11   Could there be a single love that is faithful,
that is not swayed by flattery or jewels?
The one he thinks best may often turn against him,
and the best may turn out to be the worst, at least for the soul.

15   Illicit love will always be treacherous;
Truth is clear when death is near;
All the pleasures enjoyed by then will have vanished;
only the sin is left to go on tormenting;
If he has indulged in many pleasures, he shall suffer many afflictions.

20   I should wish for a love who is ever true,
who would abet me even after life, in death.
I should gladly have such a love in life;
life in this world is brief, eternal in the other.

24   I have been around the world but I have yet to find another,
as faithful as the good Mother of God, full of grace;
no one is worthy of Her love;
let us serve Her well for she already loves us.

28   Amoriac vano dira harçaz berceguciac
     Behar handiendenian faltaturen berciac
     Vſte bano lehenguira hilcen beqhatoriac
     Harc ayuta ezpaguiça nola guiren galduyac.

32   Andre hona hardaçagun oroc gure amore
     Berce oro vci eta eguin hari ohore
     Hala eguin vadaçagu ohoratu guirate
     Berce gatic hura gabe oro galdu guirade.

36   Ieyncoaz landan mundu oroc eztu hanbat valia
     Ceruya lurra ychaſſoa haren peco gucia
     Orotara hedacendu vehar vada eſcuya
     Bera handi içan arren preciacen chipia
     Halacoa vci eta nonduquegu bercia.

41   Berce amoreac baten veci eztirade pereſtu
     Norc beria berciari eztu nahi partitu
     Ama virgen glorioſa hanbat vada conplitu
     Ororençat bera bayta leyaldela abaſtu.

45   Amoroſec badaguite vehin bere nahia
     Handiago gitençaye berce nahicaria
     Ecivqhen behinere bere conplimenduya
     Bethi peytu deramate bere mende gucia
     Emazte eta guiçonoroc har amore maria
     Eta orori vaytequegu berac conplimenduya.

51   Andre honac vqhen dici ederretan gracia
     Ehorc hura gayxteriaz ecin leçan inbia
     Bana viſtaz hilcençuyen nahicari ſaxuya
     Figuraren eqhuſtiaz daquiqueçu eguia.

55   Ychaſſoan hur gucia ceruyetan içarra
     Oyhanetan içalori lurgucian velharra
     Egunari yguzquia gau belçari ilhuna
     Lehen faltaturen dira eci hura gugana
     Balinetan eguiazqui gubagaude hargana.

28   All loves are vain but love of Her;
     the others will fail us when we need them most;
     we sinners die before we know it,
     thus if She fails to help us we are doomed!

32   Let us all take the good Lady as our love,
     Let us leave the others and honor Her!
     If we do that we ourselves shall be honored;
     Regardless of the others, without Her, we are all doomed.

36   Except for God no one else wields such power as She:
     Heaven, the earth, the sea, are all at Her feet.
     She extends Her power when needed
     Great though She is, She appreciates the humble;
     in leaving such a love, where might we find another?

41   Other loves are faithful only unto themselves;
     no one wishes to share what is his with others.
     The glorious Mother Virgin is so perfect
     that she satisfies all while remaining true.

45   If lovers have satisfied their desire,
     another greater one takes a hold thereafter.
     They may never attain full satisfaction,
     spending their whole lives in want.
     Men and women alike, take Mary as your love
     and She alone will satisfy us all fully.

51   The Good Lady alone among beauties who has had the grace
     that none can desire her unwholesomely;
     but with a single glance such unclean desires go away.
     In looking at Her image you might know this is true.

55   All the water in the sea, the stars in the sky
     Shadows in the forest, the grass upon the earth,
     The sun in the sky, darkness in the darkest night;
     all would fail us before She would
     if we would truly turn to Her.

60 Ceren bada erho guira gayxo beqhatariac
Andre leyal honegana goacen othoy guciac
Elas othoy aribira berce amore falſuyac
Harequila ſegur dugu vehar dugun gucia.

64 Elas amoros gaixoa hire enganatuya
Erhogoatan badaramac eure mende gucia
Ene andere gracioſa ezpadaquic valia
Bay bician bay hilian bethioha galduya.

68 Dembora duyan artian eguic ahal honguia
Eryoa dauguinian miraz duquec orduya
Orduyan ere nahi vaduc onſa ialguidaguia
Onſa hari gomendadi nic dioſſat eguia
Finianere eztic vzten harc galcera veria
Orduyan ere vere eſcuyan dic gracia gucia.

74 Mundu honec anhiz gende enganatu darama
Iagoyticoz vici vſtez haren ſehi dabilça
Guti vſte duyenian ehor vci darama
Erho ioqhatuy adate hartan fida dadina.

78 Ni haur ere ebiliniz anhicetan erhoric
Gaoaz eta egunaz ere hoçic eta veroric
Loa galdu pena aſqui bana ez arimagatic
Oray oro nahi nuque liren ieyncoagatic.

82 Ni beçala anhiz duçu halacoric munduyan
Mende oro dohatenic bethi vana glorian
Ohart guiten buruyari denboraden artian
Andre honac harguiçaque gomendutan aguian
Hanbat bada gracioſa ama ororen gaynian
Gindadinic eztu vzten hartu gabe gracian

88 Culpa gabe ehor ezta haur da ſegur eguia
Beqhatuyaz damnacendu iangoycoac munduya
Beqhaturic ezta yçan çutan andre handia
Ararteco çaquizcula digun varqhamenduya.

60   Why, then, are we sinners so foolish?
     Let us all turn, I pray, to this faithful Lady.
     Alas, away with all false loves!
     With Her are we sure to have all we need.

64   Alas, poor lover, how deceived thou art!
     All life long hast thou been living in foolishness.
     If my gracious Lady helps thee not,
     thou art forever doomed in life and death.

68   Do all the good thou canst whilst there is time,
     when death comes only by miracle wilt thou have another hour.
     Even then if thou still wilt do good;
     Entrust thyself fully unto Her. I am telling thee the truth:
     not even in the end does She allow damnation for Her own;
     for even then She has the fullness of grace in Her hands.

74   This world has many deceived.
     They serve it believing they will live forever,
     but they are forsaken when least expected;
     it would be madness to hazard it.

78   I myself have many a time behaved foolishly;
     Suffering through hot and cold days and nights,
     losing sleep, plenty of sorrow, but not for my soul!
     Now I should like to think it was all for God.

82   There are many like me in this world,
     all their lives caught up in vainglory.
     Let us take stock while there is time.
     The good Lady may take us under Her wing,
     so gracious is She over all other mothers;
     whoever should go to Her will not fail to receive Her grace.

88   No one is without blame, a certain truth is this.
     God condemns the world on account of its sin.
     But in Thee, noble Lady, there is no taint of sin.
     Be our intercessory that we may have His forgiveness.

92 Beccatoren ſaluaceco ieyncoac eguin cinducen
Bere buruya eguin dici iuge iuſticiaren
çu miſericordiaren refugio cinaden
Nola berac iuſtician ecin ſalualiçaque
çure miſericordiaz remedia litecen
Balinetan eguiazqui çugana gin valite.

98 Egundano ezta yçan ez içanen iagoytic
Beqhatore hayn andiric ez etare ſaxuric
Berebidian iauguin vada çuri gomendaturic
Vqhen eztuyen barqhamendu çure amorecatic
Ez galduda ez galduren çure gomenducoric
çuri gomendacen guira hilic eta viciric.

104 Berce emaztiaz ama dira cenbayt haurto chipiren
Eta guero obororic puncela ecin dirate
çu anderia ama cira virginaric ieyncoaren
Eta gueroz erreguina ceru eta lurraren.

108 Ieyncoa iaunden gauça ororen çu cirade andere
Arrazoynda mundu oroc daguien çuri ohore
Eci hala ariçaucu lheſu chriſto vera ere
çuc beçanbat dignitate mundu oroc eztuque.

112 O anderia ecin date ehor çure vardinic
Gaynecoric çuc eztuçu ieynco veraz berceric
Ieynco ezten verce oro dago çure azpitic
Ieyncoaren ama cira mundu oroz gaynetic.

116 Mundu oroc eztu eguin çuc beçanbat hargatic
Orogatic bano oboro harc ere daydi çugatic
Bere ama ecin vci obeditu gaberic
Othoy gracia eguiguçu guiren çuyenetaric.

120 Vnſa çuc harbanençaçu gomendutan gogotic
Ecin damna nayndeyela cineſtendut ſegurqui
Anhiz veguiratu duçu galduren cenetaric
Niri ere hel çaquiçat othoy galdu gaberic.

92   God made Thee for the salvation of sinners.
     He has made himself the judge of all justice
     for Thee to be a refuge for mercy.
     As He may not save them through justice,
     they shall be helped through Thy mercy,
     so long as they come unto Thee with a sincere heart.

98   There has never been, nor ever will be
     such a great and unclean sinner
     that if along the road taken he turns to Thee,
     that he is not forgiven on account of Thy love.
     No one under Thy wing has ever been damned nor ever will be.
     Unto thee do we entrust ourselves in death and life.

104 The other women are mothers of small children,
     and thereafter are they unable to be maidens.
     Thou, my Lady, being virgin, art the Mother of God,
     and thenceforth the Queen of heaven and earth.

108 Thou art Lady of all things of which God is Lord
     The world is right to render thee honor,
     for Jesus Christ himself did as much unto Thee.
     The world cannot have as much dignity as Thou.

112 My Lady, there is no one who can be Thine equal:
     Save for God Himself there is no one above Thee.
     All that is not God is below Thee;
     Thou art the Mother of God, above the whole world.

116 No one has done as much for Him as Thee;
     He has done more for Thee than all the rest;
     He can only obey His mother.
     Grant us, I pray, the grace of being Thine.

120 If Thou truly takest me under Thy wing,
     I am sure I cannot be damned.
     Thou hast protected many who would have been;
     help me too, I pray, before I am lost.

124 Ehonere gayzic ezta çuc qhen eztiroçunic
Ez etare hontaſſunic çure eſcuyan eztenic
Denbora eta leqhu orotan ecyn duda gaberic
Graciac oro çure eſcuyan iangoycoac emanic.

128 Nahi duyena hala duque amac ſemiagarric
Seme honac anhiz daydi amaren amorecatic
Gure natura haritudu çuran amoraturic
Iangoycoa ez arri duçu gure anayeturic.

132 Haren eta gure ororen ama cira digneric
Amac eztu ſofriceco ſemen artian guerlaric
Samurturic badacuxu gure gaizquiegatic
Ororen ama cira eta baqueguiçaçu bertaric.

136 Oray eguiten diraden gayzqui handiegatic
Ieyncoac ondatu çuqueyen lur gucia engoytic
Balinetan çu ezpacina ararteco gugatic
Oro ſoſtengacen guitu çure othoyegatic
Gu gayxtoac içan arren ezten çutan faltaric
Fin honera helguiçaçu guiren ſalbuyetaric.

142 Ama eztia nic badaguit çure contra faltaric
çuc gaztiga eta dreça naçaçu othoy bertaric
Elas norat ihes naydi çu neure ama vciric
Neuretaco eztaçagut çu nolaco amaric.

124 There is no evil anywhere that may not be wiped away by Thee;
nor any good which is not in Thy hands.
At all times and in all places, undoubtedly,
all grace has been given unto Thee by God.

128 A mother may obtain whatever she wants from her son;
a good son can do much for the love of his mother.
Our nature was chosen to be enthralled by Thee;
through Thee God became our brother.

132 Thou art worthy to be the Mother of God and of us all.
A mother cannot stand fighting among her children.
If Thou seest that He is angered by our iniquity,
Thou, who art the Mother of us all, reconcile us forthwith.

136 Because of the great evils being committed today,
God would have already destroyed the whole earth,
were it not for Thee mediating on our behalf;
He still spares us all thanks to Thy prayers.
Wicked though we might be, Thou art not to blame;
lead us right so that we may be saved.

142 Sweet Mother, should I fail Thee,
chide and correct me soon, I pray.
Alas, whither might I go were I to leave Thee, Mother?
I know no such mother for me like Thee.

¶Emazten fauore:

1 Emaztiac ez gayz erran ene amorecatic
Guiçonec vci valiçate elay dite faltaric.

3 Anhiz guiçon ari bada andrez gayzqui errayten
Arhizqui eta defonefqui baytituzte aypacen
Yxilica egoytia ederrago liçate
Andrec guiçonequi beci huxic ecin daydite.

7 çuhur gutic andregatic gayzqui erran diroyte
Hayez hongui erraytea oneftago liçate
Emazteac cerengatic gaiz erranendirate
Handi eta chipi oro hayetaric guirade.

11 Balentia finpleada andren gayz erraytea
Bat gayz erran nahi vadu oro vardin farcea
Yxil ladin nahi nuque halacoden gucia
Damugaycic emazteac hari eman dithia

15 Andren gayz errayle oroc bearluque penfatu
Bera eta verce oro nontic guinaden forthu
Ama emazte luyen ala ez nahi nuque galdatu
Amagatic andre oro beharluque goratu

19 Guiçonaren prouechuco emaztia bethida
Oro behin hayetaric forcen guira mundura
Sorthu eta hilguinate harc haz ezpaguiniça
Haciz guero egun oroz behar haren ayuta.

23 Haren efcuz offoan behar foynera eta iatera
Eridenian andre gabe galdu guiçon egurra
Hil badadi hura nola nordoaque gaynera
Ordu oroz behartugu ezta heben cerduda

3. In Defense of Women

1   Do not speak ill of women, for goodness' sake,
if men left them well alone, they would do no wrong.

3   If many men speak ill of ladies,
in referring to them frivolously and dishonestly,
'twould be best for them to keep silent;
women can do no wrong save with men.

7   Few wise men might speak ill of women.
'Twould be more honest to speak well of them.
Why, then, must they speak ill of women
when all of us, great and small, have been born of them?

11   Tis a foolish bit of bravado to speak ill of women,
all are lumped together when one of their kind is disparaged.
I'd much prefer such people to keep quiet.
'Tis a great pity such people were nursed by a woman!

15   All those who speak ill of women should think back
on who gave birth to him and the rest of us.
I should like to ask whether his mother was a woman or not;
he should adore all women for his mother alone.

19   A woman is always beneficial for a man;
we came into the world through them;
after our birth we should have perish had she not fed us,
and having grown up, we need her daily.

23   When in health we need a hand to clothe and feed us;
in sickness the ailing man is lost without a woman.
Should he die, who would watch over him like she does?
We undoubtedly need them every hour.

27 Emazteric ezten lecuyan eztacuſat plazeric
Ez guiçona ez echia behinere xahuric
Echianden gauça oro gayzqui erreglaturic
Parabiçuyan nahi enuque emazteric ezpaliz.

31 Emaztiac eztut ençun lehen guiçona iauquiric
Bana guiçonac emaztia bethiere lehenic
Gayxteria ialguitenda bethi guiçonetaric
Ceren bada daraucate emaztiari hoguenic.

35 Bertuteac veharluque guiçonetan handiago
Emaztetan nic dacuſſat honguiz ere guehiago
Mila guiçon gazxtoric da emaztebatendaco
Guiçon baten mila andre bere fedean dago.

39 Hec guiçoner veha valite eliçate bat honic
Eztirovte deuſcaydenic vci iauqui gaberic
Bana anhiz emazteda eſcapacen çayenic
Anderetan ceren bayta vertutea hobenic.

43 Nic eztançut emaztiac borchaturic guiçona
Bana vera çoratutic andriari darrayca
Cenbayt andre hel baledi oneriztez hargana
Ceyn guiçonec andriari emaytendu oguena.

47 Ieyncoac emaztea mayte mundu oroz gaynetic
Cerutica iayxicedin harçaz amoraturic
Emaztiac eçarridu gure anayeturic
Andre oro laudaceco haren amorecatic.

51 Irudiçayt emaztia dela gauça eztia
Donario gucietan guciz gauça emya
Gaoaz eta egunaz ere badu plazer handia
Harçaz gayzqui erraytia vilania handia.

55 Munduyan ezta gauçaric hayn eder ez placentic
Nola emaztia guiçonaren petic buluzcorriric
Beſſo viac çabalduric dago errendaturic
Guiçonorrec daguiela harçaz nahiduyenic.

27 Where there is no woman, I see nothing good;
    Neither man nor home are tidy.
    At home, disorder is the order of the day;
    I would not wish for a paradise wanting of women.

31 I have never heard of a woman striking a man first,
    rather, it is always the man who strikes the first blow.
    Wickedness always comes from men.
    Why, then, should women be blamed?

35 Virtue should be greater among men,
    for I see much more of it in women.
    There are a thousand wicked men for each woman like them,
    and a thousand faithful women for each man like them.

39 None would be honest if they looked toward men,
    for men are unable to desist from ravishing any who are good,
    but many women are able to elude their grasp,
    for their righteousness is greater.

43 I have never heard of a women violating a man.
    It is, rather, the man who madly pursues her,
    and should a woman turn to him endearingly,
    what man will fault her?

47 God loves a woman above all else in the world.
    He descended from heaven loving one of them.
    Through a woman He become our brother;
    on Her account are all women worthy of praise.

51 A woman seems to be a sweet thing to me.
    Amid all the charm she is most delicate;
    Day and night she oozes with appeal,
    to speak ill of her is villainy.

55 Nothing in the world is so beautiful or pleasurable
    as a woman under a man naked.
    With both arms stretched out, she surrenders herself
    so that the man might do with her what he will.

59 Iobadeça dardoaz ere gorpuzaren erditic
Aynguruyac bano oboro ezlarraque gayzquiric
Bana dardoa ematuric çauriere fendoturic
Bere graciaz ezarteyntu elgarrequi vaqueturic.

63 Norda guiçon modorroa harçaz orhit eztena
Eta guero halacoa gayzerrayten duyena
Ezta guiçon naturazco hala eguiten duyena
Ceren eztu eçagucen hala hongui eguina.

59 Though a bolt might tear though the middle of her,
she would complain no more than an angel.
Instead, with the bolt grown soft and the wound healed over,
her grace reconciles them both.

63 Is there anyone so callous that he forgets her,
only later to speak ill of her in such a way?
Whoever might do so is not well bred.
Why can he not recognize such a good thing?

¶Ezconduyen coplac

1   Iangoycoa edetaçu vercerena gogotic
Bera captiuada eta ni gathibu hargatic.

3   Ni gathibu naducana captiuada bercereu
Ene dichac hala eguindu ny gathibu bigaren
Gogo honez içaneniz vicy baniz bataren
Bana borchaz bayecila ez iagoytic verciaren.

7   Bercerena hardaçanac beretaco amore
Oborotan vqhenendu plazer bano dolore
Baçarriac veqhan eta veldurrequi dirate
Guti vſte dutenian gayça bertan ſordayte.

11   Honeſtea bercerena erhogoa handida
Plazer vaten vqhenendu anhiz malenconia
Beguyez icus ecin minça handacuſat nequia
Beryarequi daçanian enetaco aycia.

15   Perilequi bayecila ecin noaque hargana
Eta aguian harc orduyan ezpaytuque aycina
Baduere veldur date vertan doha harçara
Nic nahyen dudanian bercech beſſoan daraça.

19   Alhor hartan helbadaquit ereytera hacia
Eta ene vada ere laſtoa eta vihia
Ez bat ori ahalduquet ezetare vercia
Lan eguinaz eſquer gayxto galdu yrabacia
Bercerenzat gueldicenda ene çucenbidia
Aguyan guero alabarequi ezconduco ſemya.

25   Amoria ehorc ere eztu nahi partitu
Nic eztaquit berciac vana ny aryniz beqhatu
Beriarequi eqhuſtiaz hayn hayn noha penatu
Hec doſtetan ni nequetan orduyan errabiatu

4. Verses for the Married

1 Oh Lord, banish another's wife from my mind.
   She is captivated and I am captivated by her.

3 The one who captivates me is captivated by another.
   My destiny has willed that I should be captive of both.
   I shall be charmed by one as long as I live,
   but as for the other, never unless forced to.

7 He who chooses to love another's wife,
   will have more displeasure than pleasure.
   Such encounters will be few and full of fear,
   and misfortune may arise when least expected.

11 'Tis utter foolishness to love another's wife,
   for each satisfaction there will be a thousand dissatisfactions;
   I may see her, but not talk to her, what torment for me!
   And when she lies with her husband, I can only sigh.

15 I may not go where she is except at my peril,
   and then she may not have the time.
   Even if she has, she might be afraid and turn back.
   When I desire her most, the other embraces her.

19 Should I succeed in sowing the field,
   though the straw and grain might be mine,
   I may not have one or the other;
   only ingratitude for my work and what was won is lost.
   My right belongs to the other.
   And the son might even marry the daughter one day!

25 No one wishes to share his love;
   I know not about others, but in this I have sinned.
   How it pains me so in seeing her with him!
   They are frolicking, I am sulking, then raving.

29   Geloſiac eztiçaquet nic gayz erran ſeculan
       Mayte nuyena nahi enuque ehorc hunquiliaçadan
       Bercerenaz yçanuçu amoros leqhu batetan
       Beriagana geloſturic deſeſperacer ninzan

33   Amoria ecyn cençuz ecin dayte goberna
       Anhicetan honeſtendu guti vehar duyena
       Arnoac vano gayzqui ago ordidiro perſona
       Sarri eſtaca berant lacha harc hazeman deçana

37   Amoria ixuda eta eztaçagu çucena
       Eztu vſte berceric dela lecot mayte duyena
       Suyac vano gayzquiago erradiro guicona
       Ychaſſoac ez yraungui erachequi dadina.

29 I could never speak ill of jealous people.
    I would not wish for anyone to touch the one I love.
    Once I was in love with another's wife.
    I was close to despair, so jealous was I of him.

33 Love may not be bridled by common sense;
    often we love whom we should least love.
    'Tis more intoxicating for a man than any wine.
    It swiftly ties one down and only grudgingly lets go.

37 Love is blind and knows no rules.
    It believes there is none other than the one who is loved.
    It can incinerate a man more than fiercely any fire;
    no sea could put out any fire it might start.

¶Amoros fecretugui dena

1 Andre eder gentilbatec viboça deraut ebaxi
Harçaz orhit nadinian deufere ecin yrexi
Nic hura nola nahi nuque harc banença onhexi
Ecin venturatuz nago beldur daquion gayci.

5 Mirayl bat nic alhalbanu hala luyen donoa
Neure gogoa neracuxon fecretuqui han varna
Han veryan nic nacuffen harena ere nigana
Huxic ecin eguin neçan behinere hargana.

9 Ene gayzqui penaceco hayn ederric fortucen
Gaoaz eta egunaz ere gayzqui nici penacen
Harequila bat banadi vihoçazayt harricen
Neure penen erraytera are eniz aufarcen.

13 Ene gogoa balyaqui mayte vide nynduque
Nierregue valinbaninz erreguina liçate
Hura hala nahi valiz elgarrequi guinate
Haren haurrac eta eniac aurride offo lirate.

17 Valinetan nic vanerro hari neure vihoça
Eta guero valinbalit refpuefta bortiça
Dardoac vano lehen liro erdira ene vihoça
Duda gabe eror naynde han berian hilhoça

21 Artiçarrac bercetaric abantailla darama
Halaverda anderetan ni penacen nuyena
Han bat da eder eta gentil harçaz erho narama
çori honian fortu date haren beffoan daçana.

25 Ene gogoa noal vayta çucen iarri hargana
Harenere iangoycoac dacarrela nygana
Ene pena fardaquion vihocian varrena
Gogo hunez eguin daçan defiracen dudana

5. A Secret Love

1   A lovely, genteel lady has stolen my heart.
When thinking of her, I am unable to swallow.
Would that she loved me as I love her!
I dare not approach her, lest she be offended.

5   If only I had a mirror that would have such a power
that through it I could secretly show her my heart
and therein see her own thoughts toward me
In order never to cause her the least offense.

9   She was created beautiful to torment me so.
Night and day I am severely tormented
If ever I meet her, my heart is petrified with fear,
not even daring to tell her of my suffering.

13   If she only knew my mind, she would surely love me.
If I were to be king, she would be queen.
If she so wished so, we could be joined together.
Her children and mine would all be brothers and sisters.

17   If I were to tell her my heart,
and she to respond to me harshly,
quicker than any dart would my heart be rent.
I should most certainly fall dead on the spot.

21   The morning star stands out from the others;
Likewise among women she who torments me.
So fair and gentle is she that I am being driven mad.
Happily born is he who will lie in her arms.

25   As is my longing is directed toward her,
May God steer her heart to turn toward me.
To be penetrated through and through by my pain,
and gladly do as I desire.

¶Amoroſen partizia

1   Parti albanenguidio harc ezluque pareric
Alavana nic ezticit hayn hon deriçadanic.

3   Amore bat onhexi dut guciz ſoberatuqui
Ene arima eta vihoça ioſſidira harequi
Haren yrudi ederrori veguietan ehoqui
Harçaz orhit nadinian vihoza doat ebaqui.

7   Nic hargana han bat dicit amoryo handia
Harequila egoytiaz ezpaneynde enoya
Harganico particia ene eyhar garria
Berriz icus dirodano bethi malenconia.

11   Elas ene amoria nola nuçun penacen
çurequila ecin vathuz vihocian erracen
Ene gaizqui penaceco ſegur ſorthu cinaden
Penac oro honlirate çu bacina orhicen.

15   Minzaceco çurequila gaubat nahi niqueci
Hilabete conplituric hura luça valedi
Arranguren qhondaceco aſti nuyen frangoqui
Eceynere veldurgabe egoyteco çurequi.

19   Oray porogacen dicit daquitenen errana
Ehorc vci eztaçala eſcuyetan duyena
Elas yzul albaneça yraganden denbora
Segur oray enyqueci dudan gogoan veharra

23   Denbora hartan ohinicin nic çugatic dolore
Oray aldiz çure faltaz muthatuniz ny ere
Malenconya ecitela vaduqheçu amore.
Bana ordu vacinduque cençaceco çuc ere.

6. Breakup of Lovers

1   If only I could get away from her! There could be no better solution.
     But I have no other whom I love so much.

3   I have loved a woman far beyond all measure.
     My heart and soul are lashed to her;
     Her beautiful image is fixed in my eyes,
     and when I remember, my heart is rent.

7   Such is my great love for her,
     that I could not tire in her company.
     Parting from her is my withering away.
     Until I can see her again, I shall always be sad.

11   Alas, my love, what pain dost thou cause me!
     As I may not be united with thee, my heart burns.
     Thou wert truly made to torment me fearfully.
     All the sorrows would be bearable, were I in thy thoughts.

15   One night I should like to talk to thee,
     a night as long as a month,
     to tell thee of my agony at length,
     to be with thee without the slightest fear.

19   Now can I apprehend the saying of those who know:
     That nobody should give up what he has in his hands.
     Alas, if only I could bring back the time gone by!
     Then, I should not have this misgiving now.

23   At that time I would anguish over thee,
     but now, because of thee, I too have changed.
     Do not be sad, thou wilt have love,
     but it is time thou shouldst grow wise.

27 Badaquiçu doloryan partayde nyz ny ere
    Eta çure muthaceco ez oguenic batere
    Neure gayzqui penaceco harcinçadan amore
    Iagoyticoz vqhenen dut nic çugatic dolore.

27   Thou knowest, I too am in pain.
And I am not to blame for the change in thee.
I took thee as my love to suffer dreadfully.
I shall suffer forever because of thee.

¶Amoros gelofia

1   Beti penaz yçatia gayzda ene amore
     Beti ere vehar duta nic çugatic dolore.

3   Amore bat vqhen dicit miragarri gentilic
     Harequila ninçanian enuyen nic faltaric
     Nic iagoytic ecyn nuque hura veçayn mayteric
     Haren minez oray nago ecin hilez viciric.

7   Norc baytere amoria niri daraut muthatu
     Nic eztaquit cerden vana eftamendu verridu
     Ohi nola afpaldian nahi eçayt minçatu
     Cęrq andere han tuduyen vehardicit galdatu.

11   Secretuqui vehar dicit harequila minçatu
     Ordu hartan iagoyticoz exay ezpa vaquetu
     Nyri vnfa ez padaguit vehar dicit pintatu
     Ene buruya ciaydaçu harendaco abaftu.

15   Amoria nor yçanda gure bion artian
     Muthaturic vaçabilça ia afpaldi handian
     Nic çugana daquidala faltatu eztut vician
     Bioc behin fecretuqui nonbait mynça guitian.

19   Ehonere eztacuffat ni haur veçayn erhoric
     Nic norgatic pena vaytut harc ene eztu axolic
     çuhur banynz banynçande ny ere hura gaberic
     Alabana ecin vci vehin ere gogotic.

23   Gende honac vihoça daut bethiere ny garrez
     Neure amore chotiltua galdu dudan veldurrez
     Gaoaz loric ecin daydit haren gogoan veharrez
     Gogoan vehar handi dicit bethe nnyen adarrez.

7. A Jealous Lover

1   'Tis always hard to suffer, my love.
    Must I always suffer for thee?

3   I have had a love who is wonderfully charming.
    When with her, I lacked nothing.
    I could never have any love but her hereafter.
    In missing her I am living, unable to die.

7   Someone has turned my love against me.
    I know not why but her behaviour's strange.
    It has been a while since she would speak to me as she used to.
    I must ask her what has caused her to act like a haughty lady.

11   I must speak to her in secret.
    Henceforth, from that moment, we shall be friends or enemies.
    If she does me wrong, I must take to drink.
    I myself am quite capable of that.

15   My love, who has come between us?
    Thou hast long since been acting strange.
    I have, as far as I know, never in my life failed thee.
    Let us both talk somewhere in secret.

19   Nowhere do I see anyone as foolish as I;
    she, for whom I am suffering so, cares for me not.
    Were I wise, I too could do without her.
    But yet, I can never get her out of my mind.

23   Good people, my heart is forever in tears;
    out of fear that I have lost my fair beloved.
    I cannot sleep at night, so jealous am I of her.
    I greatly suspect she is being untrue to me.

27   Iangoycoa edetaçu amoria gogotic
      Eta haren yrudia ene veguietaric
      Harc nigana eztaduca vnſa leyaldateric
      Ni ere elicatu renyz oray hura gaberic
      Saroyada lohitu eta eztut haren veharric
      Nahi badut vqhenendut oray ere berriric.

27 God, erase my love from my mind,
and her image from mine eyes.
She fails to remain true to me;
I shall endure without her.
The fold is soiled and I have no need of her.
If I wish, I shall now have other loves.

¶Potaren galdacia

1   Andria ieyncoac drugaçula oray verdi guirade
      Ny erregue balinbanynz erreguina cinate
      Pot bat othoy eguidaçu ezayçula herabe
      Nic çugatic dudan penec hura merexi dute.

5   Eya horrat apartadi nor vſteduc niçala
      Horlaco bat eztuc vſte nyc icuſſi dudala
      Horrelaco hiz gaixtoric niry eztarradala
      Vercer erran albaytiça enuc vſte duyana

9   Andre gaixtoa bacinade nic eznaydi conduric
      Ciren cirena baycira çuçaz pena dicit nic
      Ene vſtian eztut erran deſoneſtaden gauçaric
      Pot bat niri eguinagatic ecinduque laydoric,

13   Hire potac bacyaquyat berce gauça nahi dic
      Anderia azticira nihaurc erran gaberic
      Bada vci albaynençac ny holacoz yxilic
      Horreyn gayz ciraden guero eguinen dut verceric.

17   Vici nyçan egunetan vada ecitut vciren
      Nic cer oray nahi vaytut heben duçu eguinen
      Vſte diat eſcuyarqui eciçala burlacen
      Guiçon hunec oray nuya heben laydoz veteren
      Eyagora nyc cer daydit çauden yxilic hanbaten.

22   Etay lelo rybay lelo pota franco vercia vego
      Andria minça albaycinde verce aldian emiago.

8. A Plea for a Kiss

1   Lady, may God protect you. Now are we on equal ground.
If I were king, you would be queen.
Please give me a kiss. Fear not!
The sorrows I have suffered for you are worthy of one.

5   Go on! Begone! Who do you take me for!
I do not think I have ever seen the likes of you.
Do not say such harsh words to me.
Go and tell the others! I am not what you take me for.

9   If you were a bad woman, I should pay no heed.
Because you are who you are, I agonize over you.
I do not believe I have said anything indecent.
By giving a kiss you would not be slighted.

13   Your kiss, I know, demands something else.
Lady, you have guessed even before I spake.
Then stop saying such things to me.
As you are so shrewish, I shall do something else.

17   As long as I live, then, I shall let you not.
That which I now desire, shall you do here.
—I truly believe you are not in jest.
—Is this man going to shame me here?
Oh, what shall I do?—Hush up a while!

22   Tralala, tralala, kisses galore and another one for good measure.
Lady, once again, speak more gently!

¶Amorez errequericia

1   Benedica fortuna ala encontru hona
     Oray beguietan dicit defiracen nuyena.

3   Ene mayte maytena eguidaçu çucena
     Ioanduçuna eqhardaçu ezpa eman ordayna

5   Nic daquidan gauçaric eztaducat çureric
     Loxaturic iarrinuçu ezpaytaquit cegatic.

7   Eztuçula veldurric eztuqueçu perylic
     Gure aucian ezta yçanen çuhaur beci iuyeric.

9   Eztut eguyn gayzquiric vqheyteco perilic
     Ez etare ceren gatic vehar dudan auciric.

11   Vada neure maytia nic dioxut eguia
     Arrobatu nuçu eta valia vequit neurya.

13   Ny enuçu ohoyna arrobaçer nyçana
     Oray othoy enadila oguen gabedifama.

15   Enetaco ohoyn cira ohoyn ere handi cira
     Nic veharren nuyen gauça daramaçu çurequila.

17   Ni enuçu iaquinxu clarqui erran eçaçu
     Ehorc vnfa adi ciçan nahi valin baduçu.

19   Guiçonac duyen maytena bay etare hobena
     Vihoceco paufuya du eta vere lo huna.

21   Oray loric ecin daydit vihocian ezpaufuric
     Hayec biac galdu ditut amoria nic çugatic.

9. A Request for Love

1   Blessed fortune! What a delightful meeting!
Now I have before mine eyes what I desired.

3   — My dearest dear, do right unto me!
Give back what thou hast taken away or else return it to me.

5   — I have nothing of thine I know of.
Thou hast frightened me and I know not why.

7   — Fear not, thou art not in peril,
at our trial shall there be no judge but thee.

9   — I have done no wrong to be in peril,
nothing for which I need a trial.

11   — Then my beloved, I shall tell thee the truth.
Thou hast robbed me and I mean to enjoy what is mine.

13   — I am no thief who goes about robbing.
Now, I pray, do not defame me if I am not guilty.

15   — For me thou art a thief, yea, a great thief.
Thou hast on thee what I need the most.

17   — I am not learned, speak clearly
if thou dost wish to be well understood.

19   — That which a man most desires, and which is his greatest possession:
Being at peace in his heart and sleeping soundly.

21   Now can I get no sleep nor rest in my heart.
These too, I have lost, my love, because of thee.

23 Vnſa penſa vedeçaçu gayzqui arrobatunuçu
   çor handian çaude eta othoy vnſa eguydaçu.

25 Galdu valin badituçu ceren oguen derautaçu
   Nic daquidan leqhutaric ni baytara eztituçu.

27 Oray egun vatetan cenaudela penſetan
   Han bat çuçaz amoratu gueroz nuçu penatan.

29 Horla erraytia errax duçu erho bocen vadaquiçu
   çura pena dioçunoc nonbayt handi videytuçu.

31 Hanbatere handituçu ecin erran nizaqueçu
   Eguiara vaciniaqui vrric ari nanguidiçu.

33 Penac handi vadituçu acheterric aſquiduçu
   Sarri ſendoturen cira larruyori oſſoduçu.

35 çauri banynz larruyan vada acheter herrian
   Ene mina ſendo ezliro çuc bayeci vician.

37 çure yrudiederrac eta mayna gentilac
   Gayzquiago çaurinici ecidardo çorroçac.

39 Vihocian çaurinuçu eta gathibatu nuçu
   Amoretan harnaçaçu nic dudana çureduçu.

41 Amexetan aguerritan ni çugatic doloretan
   Hizbat honic erradaçu hil eznadin othoy bertan.

43 Cer nahi duçu darradan gauça horren gaynian.
   Mi nolacoric aſqui duçu berceric ere herrian.

45 Verce oroz gaynetic hanbat mayte citut nic
   Mundu oro vzi niro çure amorecatic.

47 Albanerra eguya nyc dut pena handia
   Secretuqui minça guiten bioc othoy maytia.

23 In thinking back, thou hast robbed me grievously.
    Thou art greatly indebted to me, and so, I pray, be good to me.

25 — If thou hast lost these, why am I to blame?
    As far as I know, they have not come to my house from anywhere.

27 — One day, not long ago, when thou wert deep in thought,
    I fell so much in love with thee that I have been suffering ever since.

29 — In that way art thou indeed glib, thou canst play the fool well.
    The sorrows of which thou speakest seem to be truly great.

31 — So great are they that I could not tell thee of them.
    If thou didst truly know, thou wouldst take pity upon me.

33 — If thy pains are great, there are many physicians to be had.
    Thou wilt soon recover, thy skin is unscathed.

35 — If I had a flesh wound, there are physicians in the land.
    In life, nobody can heal my pain but thou.

37 Thy fair demeanour and gentle grace
    have wounded me greater than a sharp bolt could.

39 Thou hast wounded my heart and taken me captive.
    Take me in love; what is mine is thine.

41 In my dreams and daydreams I anguish over thee.
    Do say a kind word lest I should die forthwith.

43 — What wouldst thou wish me to say concerning this?
    There are plenty of others like me in the land.

45 — I love thee so much more than the others!
    I would forsake the whole world if thou wilt it.

47 If I am to tell the truth, I'm in great sorrow.
    Let the two of us, my love, talk in secret.

¶Amoroſen diſputa

1 Vztaçu hurrancera amore mayte
Oray particeco damu guinate.

3 Amoryac othoy partiguitecen
Gendiac diradela haſſi beqhaicen
Laydoc hartu gabe gueldi guitecen
Gendec yrrigarri guerta ezquiten.

7 Elas amoria ene galduya
Iamas çurequila enaynde enoya
Biciric particia pena handia
Honeyn ſarri vci nahi nuçuya.

11 Nihaurc ere guerthuz mayte bacitut
Onerizte gabez vzten eçitut
Vana ieyncoaren nuçu beldurtu
Sobera diguici eguyn beqhatu.

15 Orano amorea gazte guituçu
Ieyncuaz orhiceco leqhu diguçu
Are elgarrequi vehar diguçu
Oray particeco damu guituçu.

19 Beccatu honetan hilenbaguina
Damnatuluqueçu ene arima
Ecitela engoytic nitan engana
Nyri phoroguric eztidaçula.

23 Cineſte bat dicit gogoan honela
Nic nola daducat amore çugana
Ieyncoariere edet çaycala
Hargatic gaycexi ezquiçaquela.

10. Lovers' Quarrel

1   Let me come closer, dear love,
     'twould be a pity to leave each other now.

3   The beloved: Let us leave each other,
     for people are beginning to scorn us.
     Let us part before we are mocked,
     before we become the butt of everyone's laughter

7   Alas, my beloved, I am lost!
     I could never grow weary in thy company;
     the pain of separation while alive is great.
     Wilt thou leave me so soon?

11   — I, too, do love thee.
     I am not leaving thee for lack of love,
     but I stand in fear of God,
     so great is our sin.

15   — We are yet young, my love.
     We still have time to remember God.
     We should stay together yet.
     'Twould be a pity to leave each other now.

19   — If we died while committing this sin,
     my soul would be damned.
     Henceforth, do not entertain such notions, lest thou shouldst tempt me.

23   — There's one conviction I have in my soul which is:
     The love I have for thee
     is also pleasing to God. He cannot condemn us on that account.

27   Horlaco lauſenguz vci naçaçu
      Nola erhoturic narabilaçu
      Othoy ceniçauçu nyry euztaçu
      Ene gogoa vnſa eztacuſaçu.

31   Nola dioſtaçu horlaco hiça
      Bethi daducaçu tema borthiça
      Ioandaraudaçu lehen vihoça
      Guero gathibatu neure gorpuça

35   Horlaceco erançutez vci naçaçu
      Gueldi vacinite nahi nvqueçu
      Gure echian ohart vadaquizquigu
      Bioc iagoyticos galdu guituçu.

39   Gendiac ſo daudia bethi gugana
      Ni haurc ſecretuqui nator çugana
      çu haurc daquiqueçu noyzden ayzyna
      Neque eçayçula gitia nigana.

43   Picher ebilia hauxi diohaçu
      çucny laydo handiz vetheren nuçu
      Othoy cenyçayçu nyri vztaçu
      Niçaz axeguinic ecinduqueçu.

47   Amore maytia dioxut eguia
      çutan diagoçu ene vicia
      Nahiago dicit çure iqhuſtia
      Eci neuretaco herri gucia.

51   Horlaco lauſenguz vcinaçaçu
      Ichil vacinite nahi niqueçu
      Ieyncoaz orhiceco ordu luqueçu
      Berceric hareçaçu niri vztaçu.

55   Ieynco veldurturic iarriciraya
      Halaz deſpeditu nahi nuçuya
      Hebetic ioan gabe ene buruya
      Eguin vehar duçu ene nahia.

27 — Do not flatter me so,
thou dost baffle me so!
I beg of thee, leave me!
Thou canst not discern my inner desire.

31 — How couldst thou say such a thing?
Thou art always so steadfastly stubborn.
First didst thou steal my heart,
then didst thou seize my body.

35 — Stop making such retorts!
I wish thou wouldst stop.
If we are found out at our houses,
The two of us are lost forever.

39 — Are people always spying upon us?
I always come to thee in secret.
Thou must know it's time.
Do not trouble thyself in coming to me.

43 — "The jug passed around will eventually break upon thee."
Thou wilt bring great shame upon me.
I beg of thee, leave me be.
Thou mayst no longer take pleasure with me.

47 — Dearly beloved, I tell thee the truth;
my life is in thee.
I would rather look upon thee
than have the whole country for myself.

51 — Do not flatter me so;
I wish thou wouldst not speak.
'Tis time to think of God.
Take someone else. Leave me be.

55 — Hast thou grown fearful of God?
Wilt thou be rid of me so?
Before I go away,
must thou fulfill my desire.

59 Oray nahinuçuya heben vorchatu
    Aldi honetan othoy vci naçaçu
    Berce aldibatez ginen nyçayçu
    Nahiduçun ori orduyan daydiçu.

63 Haraycinacoric duçu errana
    Vcidaçanorrec eſcuyan du yena
    Nahi duyenian eztuqueyela
    Hiçac hari bira dugun eguyna.

67 Oray eguynduçu nahi duçuna
    Emandarautaçu ahalguey çuna
    Maradi cacendut neure fortuna
    Ceren gin vaynendin egun çugana.

71 Amore ecitela othoy deſpara
    Honat veguitartez yçul çaquicat
    Nivaytan duqueçu adiſquidebat
    Valia diquecit ſenhar gayxtobat.

59   — Now dost thou wish to take me first by force?
This time, I pray, leave me be!
I shall come to thee another time;
Then canst thou do with me what thou wilt.

63   — There is the old saying that goes:
He who lets go of what he has at hand
may not have it when he wishes.
Away with words, let us do it!

67   — Now hast thou done what thou hast wished.
Thou hast brought shame upon me.
I curse my fate
for coming unto thee this day.

71   — My beloved, despair not, I pray!
Turn around and face me this way.
Thou wilt have a friend in me
I can be as good as a bad husband for thee.

¶Ordu gayçaregui horrat zaquiçat

1   Oray vehar dnguya conquiſta verri
    Eztey yraganez gomitu handy
    Hanbat ecirade andere larri
    Merexi duçuna narçaque ſarri.

11. Begone at This Ill-Fated Moment!

1   Must we make new conquests?
Are there grand invitations after the wedding?
Thou art no such grand lady.
Soon I shall say what thou dost deserve.

¶Amore gogorraren defpita.

1   Andre eder gentilbatez hautatu çayt veguia
Herri orotan gauça oroz eztu vere paria
Othoy cebat baneguyon larradala eguia
Biderican liçatenez nynzan haren gracian

5   Refpoftuya emanderaut luçamendu gaberic
Cortefiaz honderiçut nic çuri hayn fegurqui
Berceric nitan eztuqueçu abifacencitut nic
Gazte çoroa nyçan arren enuqueçu hargatic.

9   çu gaztia bacirere adimendu hon duçu
Nic çugatic dudan pena othoy fendi eçaçu
çuretaco har nazaçu vivi nahi vanuçu
Ni çugatic hil banadi cargu handi duqueçu.

13   ohoria galcen dela plazerguitia gayz duçu
Niri horla erraytia çuri eman eztuçu
Gayxteria eguitia laydo dela daquiçu
Ny erhoa çu iaquynxu veha enaquidiçu.

17   çuhaur nahi bacirade ni fegretu nuqueçu
Gure arteco amoria ehorc eciaquiqueçu
Secretu qui minçaceco othoy bide ydaçu
Enequila minçacraz gayçiq ecin duqueçu.

21   Gayzqui eguin dadinian gendec farri daquite
Ene gayzqui eguitiaz enec laydo luqueyte
çu eta ni elgarrequi vnfa ecin guynate
çaude vxilic çoaz horrat eta hobe baitate

25   Hiz horreçaz erdiratu deraudaçu viboça
Nic çugatic dudan pena hanbat ere handida
çuçaz veraz ezpanadi oray vertan confola
Ene arima ialguirenda falta gabe canpora.

12. A Hard-Hearted Lover's Scorn

1 My eye has been struck by the sight of a fair, genteel lady.
Throughout the land there is nothing comparable to her.
I begged her to tell me the truth,
whether there might be a way to find her favor.

5 Straightaway came her response:
"You certainly have my respect out of courtesy,
you will have nothing else from me, I warn you.
A foolish girl though I might be, on that account will you not have me."

9 — Though you are young, you have good sense.
Heal, I pray, the pain I have on your account.
Make me your own if you would have me live.
Should I die on your account, you will bear a great burden.

13 — You take a fiendish pleasure while honor is being lost.
You may not speak to me in such a way.
You know it is an outrage to do wicked deeds.
I am foolish, you are learned, I shall pay no heed.

17 — If you so will, the secret stays with me
No one shall know of the love between us
Allow me to speak to you in secret
There can be no harm in speaking to me.

21 — If evil be done, people will soon know.
My family would be ashamed by my iniquity.
You and I can live well together.
Hush, begone and it will be better.

25 — With these words you have rent my heart.
So great is the sorrow which I suffer for you,
that if I am not to be consoled by you,
my soul will drift away without fail.

29 Arimaren ialguitia neque bandia duçu
Oray duçun penegatic çuria egonen duçu
Horrelaco vanitatez nyriſegur vztaçu
Prouechuric eztuqueçu eta cinhex nazaçu.

33 curequila gayzqui vaniz nola vici ninçande
Ene vihoz eta aruna çurequila dirade
Vihoz eta arima gabe ehor ecin liçate
çu eta ni elgarrequi vnſa ahal guinate

37 Iauna guerthuz hic daducat porſidia handia
Ixil endin nahi niquec ala ene ſedia
Hiz gutitan adi ezac nahi vaduc eguia
Hiretaco eztiaducat guerthuz neure buruya.

41 Hori horla liçatela nicin neure veldurra
Andriac hon deriçanari ezpadaqui meſura
Ni lehenic era guero amoros oro galdu da
Nic çuri hon vaderiçut gayzci eztaquiçula

45 Egundano yçan daya ni bay dichatacoric
Ny amoriac enu mayte nic hura ecin gaycexi
Vſte dicit narrayola ecin duquedanari
Ceren vada hori derizat hon ezteriztanari.

49 Iangoycoa mutha ezac othoy ene vihoça
Amoriaren harc veçala nic eztudan axola
Borchaz ere gavzquibano hongui eguitia hobeda
Ni haurc ere vciren dut hon ezteriztadana.

53 Andre faltaz eniz hilen valinba ni lehena
Oroz exi vehar dicit non vaytate hobena
Hequi ecin medra nayte bay gal neure arima
Bategatic ſarri niro diren oroz arnega.

29   — The departure of a soul is a great affliction.
      Yours will remain whatever the sorrow you suffer;
      cease saying such vanities to me,
      for you will gain nothing from it, I assure you.

33   — If I am at odds with you, how could I live?
      My heart and soul are with you.
      No one could live without their heart and soul,
      you and I could live well together.

37   — Milord, you are most persistent.
      In God's name, I wish you would be silent.
      In short, hear the truth if you will.
      I am truly not the one for you.

41   — I feared it would be so.
      If the woman cannot yield to the one who loves her,
      I, first and foremost, and then all lovers are doomed.
      If I do love you, take no offense.

45   To this day has there ever been anyone as hapless as I?
      My beloved loves me not and I could loathe her not.
      I believe I am pursuing someone I could never possess;
      Why, then, must I love the one who loves me not?

49   God, do change my heart
      so that I will not concern myself with such a love.
      Even when forced, it is better to do well than ill.
      I shall also leave the one who loves me not.

53   I shall not be the first to die for the lack of a woman.
      It would be best if I foreswore them all.
      I could do no good with them whereas I could lose my soul.
      I shall soon renounce all of them but for one.

¶Moſſen Bernat echaparere cantuya

1   Moſſen bernat iaquin vahu gauça nola ginenceu
Bearnora gabetaric egon ahal inçanden.

3   Heldu vehar duyen gauçan ezta eſcapaceric
Nic oguenic eznu yela hongui guitez verceric
Bide gabec haritunu vide eznuyen leqhutic
Erregueri gayzqui ſaldu guertuz oguengaberic.

7   Iaun erreguec meçu neuzan ioanenguion bertaric
Gaycez lagola ençun nuyen bana nicez oguenic
Izter beguier eneyen malician leqhuric
Ioan nendin enaguien oguen gabe iheſic.

11   Valinetan ioan ezpaninz oguenduru ninçaten
Ene contra falſeria bethi cinhexi çaten
Iuſtician ençun vaninz ſarri ialgui ninçaten
Haren faltaz haſſi nuçu iauguitiaz dolucen.

15   Vercen gayçaz cençacia çuhurcia handida
Yzterbegui duyen oro nitan vedi gaztiga
Abantallan dabilela albaylediſegura
Gayça apart egoyztea bethiere hobeda.

19   Ni gayxoa exayari ni haur giniz eſcura
Ene vnſa eguinac ere oray oro gayzdira
Haren menian ezpanengo nic nuqueyen çucena
Miraculu vanagui ere oray ene oguena.

23   Falſu teſtimoniotic ecin ehor veguira
Halaz condemnatu çuten ieyncoa erehilcera
Beccatore guira eta mira eztaquigula
Balinetan vide gabe acuſatu baguira

13. The Song of Monseigneur Bernat Etxepare

1   Monseigneur Bernat, if you had known how the matter was to be,
you might have avoided going to Beam.

3   There is no escape from what is to come,
though my only fault was doing good.
Injustice struck me whence I could not escape.
I, wrongfully betrayed to the King, was blameless.

7   My Lord the King ordered me before him without delay.
I heard he would be angry but I was innocent.
So as not to give my enemies room for malicious maneuver,
I went and ran not away, innocent though I was.

11   Had I not gone, I would have been deemed guilty.
The slander against me would have always held.
If I had been served by justice, I would have been released at once.
In absence of this, I began to regret my coming.

15   It is great wisdom to grow wise from the troubles of others.
Whoever might have an enemy be warned of my example;
let him be upon safe ground while wielding an advantage.
'Tis best to keep trouble at bay.

19   Wretched, I fell into the clutches of the enemy.
Even my good works are all now disgraced.
Had I not been under his sway, I might have been served by justice.
Now, even if I worked miracles, I would still be wrong.

23   There is no safeguard against false testimony.
Indeed they even condemned God to death.
Sinners we are and should not be surprised
when we are falsely accused.

Paciença dugun eta ieyncoac guizan ayuta
Malician dabilena verac diro mendeca.

29 Iangoycua çucirade eguiazco iugia
çure gortean vardindira handi eta chipia
Norc vaytere eguyn deraut malicia handia
Hayer hura othoy barqha niri valia eguia.

33 Iangoycoa çuc veguira exayaren menetic
Nic eniac badacuſquit ene gayçaz vozturic
çure eſcuyaz dacuſquidan heyec gaztigaturic
Ene gaynian eztaguiten vſteduten yrriric.

37 Iangoycua eguin dicit çure contrabeccatu
Hayez nahienuçula othoy heben punitu
Erregueri daquidala nic ezticit faltatu
Ceren egon vehardudan heben hanbat gatibu.

41 çuganaco huxeguinez nahi banuçu punitu
Erregue eta verce oro ene contra armatu
Gogo honez nahi dicit çure eguina laudatu
Eta exayac didan pena pacientqui haritu
Nahiz heben pena nadin arimaden ſaluatu
Hayec cer merexiduten çuhaurorrec iqhuſtzu.

47 Penac oro giten dira ieyncoaren nahitic
Eta verac permiticen oro hobenagatic
Aguian hula ezpanango hil ninçanden engoytic
Ene exayac galdu vſtian ene hona eguindic.

51 Berac baçu hil dirade ni are nago viciric
Hongui eguin vſte vaytut ohorezqui ialguiric
Gayça nola hona ere iauguinenda vertaric
Gayz eqhuſſi eztu yenac hona cerden eztaqui.

55 Hongui eguitez gayz ſofrituz vehardugu ſaluatt
Pena eta miſeria nic enuyen daſtatu
Oray daquit iangoycuac enu nahi damnatu
Heben ene penacera çaydanyanorhitu
Vrhe hunac vehardici ſuyan vnſa purgatu.

Let us be patient and God help us.
He can take vengeance upon whomever wallows in wickedness.

29   Lord, Thou art the judge of truth.
The great and the small are equal in Thy court.
Someone has done me a great wrong.
Forgive them, I pray. My defense is truth.

33   Lord, preserve me from the grasp of the enemy,
I can see mine taking delight in my misfortune.
May I see them smitten by Thy hand,
that they might not mock me for whatever they think.

37   Lord, I have sinned against Thee.
Punish me not me for them now.
For all I know I have committed no fault against the King.
Why must I remain here captive for so long?

41   If Thou wilt punish me for the sins I committed against Thee,
to turn the King and all the others against me,
I sincerely wish to praise Thy work,
to bear patiently the anguish the enemy inflicts upon me,
in the hope by suffering, my soul might be saved.
Thou thyself wilt see what they deserve.

47   All suffering emanates from the will of God,
and He allows them all for the greatest good.
Perhaps were I not in this plight, I should be dead by now.
My enemy, thinking me doomed, has done me some good.

51   Some of them are dead; yet I continue to live,
hoping to do good when I am honorably released.
Good, like evil, will also come to the fore:
Whoever has seen no evil knows not what good is.

55   We must save ourselves by doing good, by suffering evil.
I had not tasted of sorrow and misery.
Now I know: God did not wish to punish me
when He thought of having me suffer here:
Fine gold must be purified by fire.

60   Vere nahi ezpanindu eninduquen punitu
     Aytac vere haur maytia gaztigatu ohidu
     Bihi hunac gorde gabe vehardici xahutu
     Iangoycoac nizaz ere hala aguian eguindu.

64   Moſſen bernat penſa ezac carcel hori gayzbada
     Nonbayt ere yfernuya are gayçago dela
     Heben hic vaduquec vana hayecez norc conſola
     Penac heben findic ſarrihayenac ez ſeculan.

68   Vatre minic heben eztuc lecot ialgui nahia
     Handirenec bethidie ſuyan pena handia
     Pena handi ycigarri eceyn pauſu gabia
     Harçaz orhit adi eta duquec paciencia.

72   Vercen gaztigari inçan oray adigaztiga
     Penahonez orhit eta hangoezac cogita
     Heben goaz vercecoa albaheça eſcuſa
     Vnſa enplegatu duquec heben eure denbora.

76   Horbalego gaztigayro ihaurc verce gucia
     Bada oray gaztiguezac aldiz eure burya
     Quiryſayluyari nola hiri hel eztaquia
     Bercer argui eguin eta erracendic buruya.

80   Hiri eguin vadarye bide gabe handia
     Ieyncoari gomendezac eure gauça gucia
     Harc ororiemanendic bere merexituya
     Gayzqui guiler pena handi pacienter gloria.

84   Eztaçala gayzeriztez damna heure buruya
     deſiratuz gayxtoariheldaquion gazquia
     Ieyncuari eguitenduc in iuria handia
     Hura borrer eguitenduc iuge eure buruya.

88   Certan iuya hic vaytaçac eure yzterbeguia
     Hartan condemnacen duquec yhaurc eure buruya
     Eta hartan eztaquidic eſcuſaric valia
     Eracuſtac ehonere norden oguen gabia.

60   If He did not want me as His, He would not punish me.
The father disciplines the child he loves.
The good grain must be cleaned before being stored away.
God may have done the same for me as well.

64   Monseigneur Bernat, just think, if this prison is bad,
hell is likely to be even worse.
Here you have someone to console you, those below do not.
Your sorrow will soon be over here but theirs will not.

68   Here you suffer no pain save for the desire to flee.
The ones below are always suffering a great, fiery sorrow.
A great, terrible, never-ending sorrow.
Remember that and you will have patience.

72   You were an adviser to others and now you are being advised.
When remembering this suffering, think of those down there.
If you are able to avoid the one down there while up here,
you will have spent your time up here well.

76   You yourself would know how to advise anyone were he there.
Now then, take some advice yourself,
so that what happens to a candle will not happen to you:
Having given light to others, it burns itself out.

80   If they have done you a great wrong,
put your case in God's hands.
He will give each one his just rewards:
Great anguish to those who do evil, glory to those who are patient.

84   Do not condemn yourself through spite,
in wishing that evil should happen to the wicked.
You are doing God a great injustice.
You are making him a hangman and yourself a judge.

88   Where you have judged your enemy,
there have you condemned yourself,
and there will no excuse suffice.
Show me anyone anywhere who is without sin.

92 Iangoycua oray dicit eguiteco handia
Hiri honetan eryocez hilcenduçu gendia
Gathi butan hil enadin guiçon oguen gabia
Oſſoric othoy ialguiteco çuc ydaçu vidia
Izterbeguiac eztaguidan guibeletic irria
Oguenduru çuyan eta hangaldudic vicia.

98 Libertatia nola vayta gaucetaco hobena
Gathi butan egoytia hala pena gaycena
Ny veçala eztadila othoy ehor engana
Ez etare hiz orotan fida ere guiçona
Iaygoycuaçuc veguira niri ere çucena.
Amen.

92   God, I now have a great task.
      In this city many are being murdered.
      Lest I should die in captivity, an innocent man,
      give me, I pray, the wherewithal to come out a healthy man
      so that my enemy will not later chuckle:
      "He was guilty and there he lost his life."

98   As freedom is the greatest of things,
      captivity is the worst kind of suffering.
      Let no person be fooled, I pray, as I was.
      Nor let any man trust every word.
      My God, defend my right.
      Amen.

¶Contrapas

1   Heuſcara ialgui adi cãpora

2   Garacico herria
Benedica dadila
Heuſcarari emandio
Beharduyen thornuya.

6   Heuſcara
Ialgui adi plaçara

8   Berce gendec víteçuten
Ecin ſcribaçayteyen
Oray dute phorogatu
Euganatu cirela.

12   Heuſcara
Ialgui adi mundura

14   Lengoagetan ohi inçan
Eſtimatze gutitan
Oray aldiz hic beharduc
Ohoria orotan.

18   Heuſcara
Habil mundu gucira

20   Berceac oroc içan dira
Bere goihen gradora
Oray hura iganenda
Berce ororen gaynera.

24   Heuſcara

14. Contrapas

1   Basque,
        go forth into the world!
    Blessed be the land of Garazi;
    For it has given Basque the rank it deserves.
        Basque,
        go forth into the street!

8   Other people thought
    it could not be written;
    now they have seen
    that they were wrong.
        Basque,
        come forth into the world!

14 Among tongues wert thou
    held in low esteem;
    but now thou art due
    honor among them all.
        Basque,
        come forth into the whole world!

20 All the others
    are at their zenith.
    Now Basque shall rise
    above all the others!
        Basque!

25 Baſcoac oroc preciatzẽ
Hueſcara ez iaquin harrẽ
Oroc iccaſſiren dute
Oray cerden heuſcara.

29 Heuſcara

30 Oray dano egon bahiz
Imprimitu bagueric
Hi engoitic ebiliren
Mundu gucietaric.

34 Heuſcara

35 Eceyn ere lengoageric
Ez franceſa ez berceric
Oray ezta erideyten
Heuſcararen pareric.

39 Heuſcara
Ialgui adi dançara.

25   All hold Basques in esteem
      though they know Basque not.
      Now all will learn
      what Basque is.
          Basque!

30   If hitherto thou hast been
      unprinted,
      henceforth shalt thou speak
      throughout the world.
          Basque!

35   For no language shall be found,
      be it French or any other,
      to be the equal of Basque.
          Basque,
              go forth and dance!

¶Sautrela

1 Heuſcara da campora, eta goacen oro dançara

2 O heuſcara laude ezac garacico herria
Ceren hantic vqhen baytuc beharduyan thornuya
Lehenago hi baitinçan lengoagetan azquena
Oray aldiz içaneniz orotaco lehena.

6 Heuſcaldunac mundu orotan preciatu ciraden
Bana hayen lengoagiaz berceoro burlatzen
Ceren eceyn ſcripturan erideiten ezpaitzen
Oray dute iccaſſiren nolagauça honacen.

10 Heuſcaldun den guiçon oroc alchabeça buruya
Ecihuyen lengoagia içanenda floria
Prince eta iaun handiec oroc haren galdia
Scribatus halbalute iqhaſteco deſira.

14 Deſir hura conplitu du garacico naturac
Eta haren adiſquide oray bordelen denac
Lehen imprimiçalia heuſcararen hurada
Baſco oro obligatu iagoiticoz hargana

18 Etay lelori baïlelo leloa çaray leloa
Hueſcara da campora eta goacen oro dançara.

DEBILE PRINCIPIVM MELIOR
FORTVNA SEQVATVR

15. Sauterelle

1   Basque has come forth and let us all go and dance.

2   O Basque, praise the town of Garazi,
for thence hast thou attained the rank thou deservest.
If before thou wert last among tongues,
now art thou above them all.

6   The Basques are appreciated the world over,
but all the rest have mocked their tongue,
for it was not found written on any page.
Now shall they learn what a fine thing it is.

10   Every Basque should hold his head high,
for his language shall be the flower
for which Princes and great lords shall ask.
They will desire to learn it and, if able, write it.

14   A man born in Garazi has fulfilled this desire
as well as his friend in Bordeaux.
He is the first printer of the Basque tongue;
to him are all Basques indebted forever.

18   And tralala, tralala, falalalala!
Basque is now out and about and let us go to the dance!

OUT OF A HUMBLE BEGINNING
MAY BETTER FORTUNE FOLLOW

¶Extraict des regeftes de Parlement.

Svpplie humblement Françoys Morpain, maiftre Impimeur de cefte ville de Bourdeaulx, que pour imprimer vn petit tracte intitule, Linguæ vafconum primitie, luy a conuenu faire plufieurs fraiz & mifes. A cefte caufe plaife a la Court inhibitions eftre faictes a tous les Imprimeurs libraires de ce Reffort de imprimer ou faire imprimer ledict Tracte, & a tous marchãs de nen vendre dautre impreffion dans troys ans a peine de mil liures tourñ. & ferez iuftice. Veue laquelle requefte la court faict les inhibitions requifes par ledict Morpain a peine de mil liures tourñ. Faict a Bourdeaulx en Parlement le dernier iour Dapuril, mil cinq cens quarante cinq.

Collation eft faicte.

De Pontac.

Extract from the Registry

Francois Morpain, master printer of this city of Bordeaux hereby humbly makes the following request: in printing the booklet entitled *Linguæ Vasconum Primitiæ*, he has had to undergo great expense and costs. In consideration thereof, may it please the Court to forbid every book printer in this jurisdiction to print or have printed said booklet, and forbid every merchant to sell any other printing thereof for three years under the penalty of a thousand Tours pounds.

In consideration of this petition, the Court has hereby granted by decree the bans requested by said Morpain under penalty of a thousand Tours pounds.

Delivered in Bordeaux at Parliament, the last day of April, fifteen hundred and forty-five.

Request granted
De Pontac

Suggestions for Further Readings

This short list of suggested reading is intended to orient the nonspecialist reader toward Bernard Etxepare and his contemporary world. It consists of three sections: contemporary related works, some selected general bibliography on Etxepare, and an introductory list of mostly contemporary works on Basque history and culture that relates to the broad themes discussed in the present work and is weighted toward English-language studies.

Selected Works Contemporary to Etxepare

Axular [Pedro de Aguerre]. *Guero bi partetan partitua eta berezia . . .* Bordeaux: Guillen Milanges, 1643. Reprint, facsimile edition. Bilbo: Euskaltzaindia, 1988.

Leiçarraga, Ioannes [Joannes Leizarraga]. *Iesust Christ gure Iaunaren Testamentu berria..* La Rochelle: Pierre Hautin, 1571. Reprint, facsimile edition of Theodor Linschmann and Hugo Schuchardt's 1900 edition. Bilbao: Euskaltzaindia, 1990.

Madariaga Orbea, Juan, ed. *Anthology of Apologists and Detractors of the Basque Language.* Translated by Frederick H. Fornoff, María Critina Saavedra, Amaia Gabantxo, and Cameron J. Watson. Reno: Center for Basque Studies, 2006.

Oihenart, Arnaud. *Notitia utriusque Vasconiæ, tum Ibericæ, tum Aquitanicæ . . .* Paris: Sebastian Cramoisy, 1638. Reprint, facsimile edition. Translation of Latin text by Javier Gorosterratzu. With an introduction by Ricardo Cierbide. Vitoria-Gasteiz: Eusko Legebiltzarra/Parlamento Vasco, 1992.

Rabelais, François. *The Complete Works of Rabelais: The Five Books of Gargantua and Pantagruel.* New York: The Modern Library, 1944. Among many editions in English and French.

Ruiz, Juan. *El libro de buen amor.* Many editions. In English: *The Book of Good Love.* Translated by Elisha Kent. Newark, DE: Juan de la Cuesta Hispanic Monographs, 2005.

Selected Bibliography on Bernard Etxepare

Altuna, Francisco [Patxi]. *Etxepareren hiztegia: Lexicon dechepariano.* Bilbao : Mensajero, 1979.

―――. *Versificación de Dechepare: Métrica y pronunciación.* Bilbao: Mensajero, 1979.

Arcocha-Scarcia, Aurélie. "Les *Linguæ Vasconum primitiæ* de Bernard Dechepare." In *Les voix de la nymphe d'Aquitaine: Ecrits, langues et pouvoirs, 1550–1610.* Edited by Jean-François Courouau, Jean Cubelier, and Philippe Gardy. Agen: Centre Mateo Bandello, 2005.

Aulestia, Gorka. "Bernard Detxepare – Medieval or Renaissance Writer?" In *The Basque Poetic Tradition.* Translated by Linda White. Foreword by Linda White. Reno: University of Nevada Press, 2000.

Haritschelhar, Jean. "Défense et illustration de la langue basque au XVIe siècle: La *Sautrela* de Bernat Echapare." *Hommage à Jacques Allières, I. Domaine basque et pyrénéen,* edited by Michel Aurnague and Michel Roché Anglet. Biarritz: Atlantica, 2002.

Madariaga Orbea, Juan. "Bernard Dechepare." In *Anthology of Apologists and Detractors of the Basque Language,* edited by Juan Madariaga Orbea. Translated by Frederick H. Fornoff, María Critina Saavedra, Amaia Gabantxo, and Cameron J. Watson. Reno: Center for Basque Studies, University of Nevada, Reno, 2006.

Orpustan, Jean-Baptiste. *Précis d'histoire littéraire basque, 1545–1950. Cinq siècles de littérature en euskara.* Baigorri: Izpegi, 1996.

Urrutia, Andrés. "Bernat Etxepare, el poeta de una lengua sin Estado." In *Los escritores: hitos de la literatura clásica euskerica,* edited by Gorka Aulestia. Vitoria-Gasteiz : Fundación Sancho el Sabio, 1996.

Selected Bibliography on Basque History and Culture

Aulestia, Gorka. *The Basque Poetic Tradition.* Translated by Linda White. Foreword by Linda White. Reno: University of Nevada Press, 2000.

Barandiarán, José Miguel de. *Selected Writings of José Miguel de Barandiarán: Basque Prehistory and Ethnography.* Translated by Fredrick H. Fornoff, Linda White, and Carys Evans-Corales. Compiled and with an introduction by Jesús Altuna. Reno: Center for Basque Studies, University of Nevada, Reno, 2007.

Caro Baroja, Julio. *The Basques.* Translated by Kristin Addis. With an introduction by William A. Douglass. Reno: Center for Basque Studies, University of Nevada, Reno, 2009.

Collins, Roger. *The Basques.* Oxford: Basil Blackwell, 1986.

Douglass, William A., ed. *Essays in Basque Social Anthropology and History.* Reno: Basque Studies Program, University of Nevada, Reno, 1989.

Douglass, William A., and Joseba Zulaika. *Basque Culture: Anthropological Perspectives.* Reno: Center for Basque Studies, University of Nevada, Reno, 2007.

Gallop, Rodney. *A Book of the Basques.* 1930. Reprint, Reno: University of Nevada Press, 1970.

Henningsen, Gustav. *The Witches' Advocate: Basque Witchcraft and the Spanish Inquisition.* Reno: University of Nevada Press, 1980.

Lagarde, Anne-Marie. *Les basques: Société traditionnelle et symétrie des sexes; Expression sociale et linguistique.* Preface by Txomin Peillen. Paris: L'Harmattan, 2003.

Mitxelena, Koldo. *Koldo Mitxelena: Selected Writings of a Basque Scholar.* Translated by Linda White and M. Dean Johnson. Compiled and with an introduction by Pello Sallaburu. Reno: Center for Basque Studies, University of Nevada, Reno, 2008.

Monreal Zia, Gregorio. *The Old Law of Bizkaia (1452): Introductory Study and Critical Edition.* Translated by William A. Douglass and Linda White. Preface by William A. Douglass. Reno: Center for Basque Studies, University of Nevada, Reno, 2005.

Ott, Sandra. *The Circle of the Mountains: A Basque Shepherding Community.* 1981. Reprint, Reno: University of Nevada Press, 1993.

Salaburu, Pello, and Xabier Alberdi, eds. *The Challenge of a Bilingual Society in the Basque Country.* Reno: Center for Basque Studies, 2012.

Veyrin, Philippe. *The Basques of Lapurdi, Zuberoa, and Lower Navarre: Their History and Their Traditions.* Translated by Andrew Brown.

With an introduction by Sandra Ott. Reno: Center for Basque Studies, University of Nevada, Reno, 2011.

Watson, Cameron. *Modern Basque History*. Reno: Center for Basque Studies, 2003.

Xamar [pseudonym, Juan Carlos Etxegoien]. *Orhipean: The Country of Basque*. Translated by Margaret L. Bullen. Pamplona: Pamiela, 2006.

Zulaika, Joseba. *Del cromañon al carnival: Los vascos como museo antropológico*. Donostia: Erein, 1996.

Index of Poems and First Lines